FINE
CHEESE

FINE
CHEESE

Written by Leonie Glass
Consultant editor Arthur Cunynghame

Photography by Geoff Dann

Kyle Cathie Limited

This new revised 2009 edition published by
Kyle Cathie Limited
122 Arlington Road, London NW1 7HP
general.enquiries@kyle-cathie.com
www.kylecathie.com

Conceived, designed and produced by
Duncan Petersen Publishing Ltd
C7, Old Imperial Laundry, Warriner Gardens,
London, SW11 4XW

ISBN 978-1-85626-887-5

Consultant editor Arthur Cunynghame
Designer Ian Midson
Editor Helen Warren
Additional text by Caroline Cheek and
Sophie Steele
Studio photography by Geoff Dann
Editorial director Andrew Duncan
With thanks also to Ros Windsor, Richard
Sutton and staff at
Paxton & Whitfield
Colour reproduction by
Universal Graphics, Singapore;
The Colourhouse, UK
**Printed by Star Standard Industries Pty Ltd,
Singapore**

FOREWORD

'Selective' - by which we mean picking out the best – is regarded by some as a dirty word these days, but this book is unashamedly so.

In picking out the 200 European cheeses we think are, simply, the best, we have not only relied on our instincts. We have chosen, of course, most of the AOC cheeses, and those with long reputations for consistent quality, both of which are reasonably objective measures.

More important, perhaps, we have favoured the small, 'craft' cheese makers – also known as 'farmhouse' or artisan producers – over larger scale or 'industrial' producers. Such individuals are able to make cheeses full of character reflecting the area in which they are made, the herbage on which the animals have grazed and, not least, the skills of the cheese maker himself. Larger businesses with their commercial requirements of shelf life, price and uniformity of flavour are seldom able to produce cheeses of truly superb quality.

If there is a bias in our selection, it is in trimming the number of cheeses featured from cheese giants such as France, Britain, Spain and Italy, in order to include cheeses from countries which produce less such as Norway and Sweden. Cheeses from such lesser producers are sometimes very good, sometimes not as good as others elsewhere in this book, but still worth featuring because they represent the best from that particular country.

Any list of cheeses remains at heart subjective; not least because cheeses vary in quality from one maker to another, from season to season and indeed from day to day; but we believe we will have done our job if, from reading this book, you discover just one new cheese that you enjoy enough to tell others about.

Leonie Glass
Arthur Cunynghame

CONTENTS

INTRODUCTION

The world of cheese, past and present.

The first cheese makers of prehistoric times; cheese in Greek and Roman times; and the development of modern cheese.

How cheese is made and classified, and, perhaps more important to enjoying cheese, how it changes not only according to the type of milk used and the way its made, but also with the seasons.

Practical advice on looking after cheese; how to put together a cheeseboard; what cheese to serve with different foods; what wine to drink with cheese; and finally cheese accessories.

ABOUT THIS BOOK

Organization

Pages 12-37 comprise a general introduction, with information on the history of cheese making, modern production methods and serving suggestions.

Following this is the main part of the book, 17 country sections, not in alphabetical order. The big cheese producing countries come first. Smaller producers follow, arranged geographically. Within each country, we generally follow an alphabetical order.

Half page entries

Each of the cheeses we have selected deserves at least half a page of text and a full colour specially commissioned photograph.

Full page entries

These are cheeses which Arthur Cunynghame and Leonie Glass believe stand out as the best gourmet experiences. We feel that they merit a fuller description of production methods, taste and accompaniments.

Terminology

There is a wealth of technical terms related to cheese which may, at first, seem confusing to the casual observer. The glossary opposite defines the most important terms used in this book. Others are listed in the index and explained within the text.

GLOSSARY

Affinage the period of time that a cheese spends ripening or maturing.

Affineur highly skilled person who oversees the maturation process.

Artisanal similar to *fermier*, artisan type small-scale production of cheese.

Brining washing a cheese with saltwater to promote formation of a rind.

Casein label label made of the principal milk protein, casein.

Coagulation the process by which curds and whey are separated, using an agent.

Cooking heating a cheese to 45-50°C as part of the production process.

Cooperative several farmers 'pool' their milk to make cheese together.

Fat in dry matter amount of fat in a cheese expressed as the percentage of fat in cheese if all water were removed.

Fermier the production of cheese in traditional farmhouse ways, often on a relatively small scale. See *Industriel*.

Fourme The mould a cheese is made in.

Industriel industrial scale production of cheese. See *Fermier*

Pâte sometimes referred to as paste, this describes the interior of the cheese.

PDO Protected Designation of Origin. New EU-wide system of standards.

Penicillium a mould that often grows or on the rind of a cheese. It gives cheeses such as Camembert their white, fluffy appearance.

Raw/unpasteurized is milk in its natural state.

Rennet enzyme used to aid coagulation.

Rind may be washed or natural rind; the former may be washed in a great variety of liquids, including Marc, whisky or wine, or frequently in brine.

CHEESE IN HISTORY

The northern European words cheese, *kaas* and *käse* and the Iberian words *queso* and *queijo* are all derived from the Latin word caseus which refers to the wicker basket in which cheese was left to drain. Interestingly, the Italian and French words *formaggio* and *fromage* come directly from the Greek word *formos*, also meaning basket or container. The Scandinavian word *ost* probably comes from the same root.

First cheese makers

No one really knows where or when people first started making cheese, but it was certainly many thousands of years ago. We do know that sheep were domesticated around 12,000 years ago, and that some time later both sheep and cows were raised in Sumer and ancient Egypt. It seems reasonable to suppose that around that time people discovered that if milk was left in the warmth of the sun it would sour and separate into white solids in a watery liquid. It only needed the liquid to be drained off to produce a primitive kind of fresh cheese. Similar discoveries were probably made with yak's milk in Mongolia and camel's milk in Africa. It takes little imagination to realize how significant the discovery must have been to early people whose chances of survival when food was scarce could be enhanced by this self-preserving source of fat and protein.

The next step forward was the use of rennet to separate the curds and whey. The story goes that a shepherd found that the milk he was carrying in his leather container had turned into solids. Rennet, an enzyme secreted from the lining of a calf's stomach, produces a

SIGNIFICANT DATES

12,000 BC	Domestication of sheep and possible start of fresh cheese making by natural souring.	1851	First Cheddar cheese factory opens in America.
7000-5000 BC	First cheeses made with the use of rennet to curdle the milk.	1910	Registration of Stilton as a trade mark.
2000 BC	Sophisticated range of Greek cheeses developed.	1925	Recognition of Roquefort as a cheese unique to its region.
1000 BC	Roman soldiers spread cheese making throughout the empire.	1939	Farmhouse cheese production severely curtailed by rationing in the U.K.
50 AD	Pliny the Elder writes about French cheeses.	1958	First full AOC status for a cheese awarded to Comte in France.
850s	Dutch cheese is sent to the court of Charlemagne.	1980s	Renaissance of farmhouse cheese making in the U.K.
1100s	First written mention of Gruyère cheese.	1990s	Introduction of Europe-wide PDO cheeses.
1500s	Cheese making starts to move from monasteries to farms.	2000s	Growth of farmhouse cheese making in U.S.A. and Australia.
1850s	Louis Pasteur invents pasteurization.		

HARD AND SOFT

Medieval cheese fell into three categories: hard, semi-soft and soft. Hard cheese made from skimmed milk was destined for servants, farm workers and peasants. In Britain, it was well known that the worst of the hard cheeses came from East Anglia. A rude little rhyme about cheese made in the East Anglian county of Suffolk ran:

Those that made me were uncivil
They made me harder than the devil
Knives won't cut me, fire won't sweat me
Dogs bark at me, but can't eat me

curd that is firmer and less bitter than that produced simply by leaving the milk out to sour in the sun.

As time went on, people who lived near the sea or salt plains found that mixing salt into the curd resulted in cheese with a much longer life. Others found that using baskets or porous pottery to store the cheese resulted in better drainage. Moulding and pressing techniques were added to the cheese maker's repertoire. However, there is no written record of this progression until the Greek age, when cheese making was already diverse and quite sophisticated.

Cheese in Greek and Roman times

The Greeks enjoyed fresh cheese at home and made hard cheese which they traded around the Mediterranean. However, it was the Romans who introduced cheese to the farthest corners of their world. Soldiers received a daily ration of cheese, so wherever a fort was established cheese making would follow. The Romans also taught the art of cheese making to the tribes of north-western Europe, and local cheeses such as Roquefort and Cantal became highly sought after in Rome itself. In Britain, Roman soldiers are said to have hanged a cheese maker in Chester for refusing to give them the recipe for Cheshire cheese.

After the fall of the Roman Empire, cheese making went into decline, but the monastic orders ensured that it did not die out altogether. Then, in the Middle Ages, the need for cheese started to grow again. It was eaten on the many feast days, and by certain religious orders who were forbidden meat. Monasteries started to develop their own distinctive cheeses, and eventually to teach local farmers the techniques needed to make them. Many monastery-style cheeses survive to this day, for example Etrammes, Munster, Livarot and Maroilles from France and Hervé from Belgium.

Development of modern cheese

It was not until the 19th Century that these local cheeses began to be available outside their own regions; until then, cheese making remained a small-scale and labour-intensive art. Then, in the late

Opposite: weighing cheese
Weighing has always been part of the ritual of buying cheese. During the Middle Ages, the importance of cheese making in the Low Countries saw the development of specialist cheese markets and cheese weigh houses, or *kaaswaag*, which were concerned with quality control. All the cheeses were inspected for quality and weight. The *kaaswaag* in Gouda carries a fine relief above the door showing how the cheeses were weighed.

WATER BUFFALO CHEESE
Water buffalo wallowing in southern Italy. No one quite knows how the animals first arrived there. One theory is that they came with the Longobards around 596 AD. Alternatively, they may be indigenous to the region. Until the beginning of the 19th Century, herds of buffalo roamed the countryside in a semi-wild state, being gathered at dawn for milking. The milk was used to make Mozzarella and is still the best for this purpose.

19th Century, the invention of scientific methods of testing acidity and of pasteurizing milk to remove micro-organisms allowed much larger-scale production.

When the Europeans colonized the New World, they took their cheese making skills with them, but, as elsewhere, production was localized and small-scale until Jesse Williams opened the first Cheddar cheese factory in Oneida County, New York State in 1851. Many of the early settlers in Australia and New Zealand were British, and Cheddar became the main prototype in the Antipodes. In America, Colby, Monterey Jack and Tillamook are all variations of Cheddar.

Factory production of cheese was gradually developed to such an extent that after the Second World War mechanization almost completely replaced artisan production in many of the northern European countries.

In France and Italy this changeover was much slower and not so far-reaching, but large factory-like creameries have still taken over a quite a large percentage of cheese production. You can tell quite simply which French cheeses are still produced in the traditional way by looking on the label for the terms *fermier* meaning farm produced and *laitier* meaning factory produced.

ABOVE: THE BELL INN AT STILTON

Stilton was first mentioned in 1725 by the English novelist Daniel Defoe when he was touring England and Wales and sampled the cheese in the village of Stilton. In fact, Stilton was never actually made in the village, though it came to fame at the Bell Inn. Tradition has it that the recipe for

Stilton was developed at Quenby Hall in Leicester. The housekeeper at the hall passed it on to her daughter, Mrs Frances Paulet, who then supplied the Bell Inn. In 1910, Stilton was registered as a trademark and its production limited to Derbyshire, Nottinghamshire and Leicestershire.

How cheese is made

The principles of cheese making are the same for all but the simplest of fresh cheeses. Milk is prepared and coagulated so that the water or whey can be extracted from the milk, leaving the milk solids or curds behind. The curds are cut and moulded and may be salted and pressed to form cheeses which are then ripened by storing for a while. Within these principles there is room for endless variation and this is where the cheese maker's art comes in. Over the years their skills and their interest in experimentation have resulted in hundreds of different cheeses.

Collecting and preparing the milk

Milk from almost any animal can be used to make cheese, but the most common is cow's milk followed by sheep and goat's milk. Sometimes cream is added to make a richer cheese, or cream may be partially removed by skimming to make a lower fat cheese.

In the past, only raw milk was used for cheese making and the very best cheeses are still made in this way. We tend to think of milk as just milk, but the food the animal eats, the soil on which the pasture grows and even the weather on the day the animal is milked all have an effect on the taste of the milk and so on the taste of the cheese. There is a difference between summer and winter milk, spring and autumn milk, morning and evening milk and even between milk obtained at the start of milking and at the end. The cheese maker will take all of these elements into account when making the cheese.

Today, large quantities of cheese are made with pasteurized milk which has been heat-treated to kill off any potentially harmful bacteria that might be

OPPOSITE: CATTLE IN THE AUSTRIAN ALPS
Different breeds of cattle produce very different flavours of milk. The French, particularly, recognize this and in many regions the breed of animal for a specific cheese is laid down in law. For example, Reblochon is made with milk from the small Montbéliard cows indigenous to Savoie. The regulations for Beaufort and for Fourme d'Ambert require not only that the milk should come from indigenous cows, but that their feed should also come from within the AOC region.

ABOVE:
GOATS GRAZING IN THE AUSTRIAN ALPS
Goats are even hardier than sheep (see
page 25), highly omnivorous, and can tol-
erate sparse, rocky grazing. However,
they can also thrive on the fat of the
land, and the goats that produce many of
the most famous cheeses (for example,
Loire Valley Chevre) are contented, well-
fed farm animals.

present. The pasteurization process is useful to large producers because it allows them to standardize milk from many different suppliers. It also gives them more control over the cheese making process. The result is a uniform product which is consistently clean and pleasant. The disadvantage is that the process tends to destroy the individual character of the cheese. EU law allows raw milk in cheese making; and as this book went to press, only Denmark banned raw milk in cheese.

Producing the curds

When the milk comes into the dairy or creamery, it is poured into large containers where it may be pasteurized or be given additives such as cream or natural dyes such as annatto.

A special 'starter culture' of carefully chosen bacteria is added to the milk. This increases the acidity level of the milk by changing the milk sugars or lactose into lactic acid, making it easier for the milk to form curds when a coagulating agent is added. Cheese makers constantly measure the acidity level of the milk so that they know exactly the right moment to add the coagulating agent, normally rennet. Once this has been added, the protein or casein molecules in the milk lump together to form a soft, jelly-like mass.

Cutting and treating the curds

After 30 minutes to two hours, depending on the cheese being made, the curds are cut. The way in which the curds are cut determines the texture of the finished cheese. Light cutting releases less whey and results in a softer cheese. The curds for cheeses such as Camembert and Brie are hardly cut at all; instead they are immediately spooned into moulds and left to drain naturally.

Heavy cutting, sometimes both vertically and horizontally, results in much harder cheeses. The small pieces of curd fall to the bottom of the vat and cling together again to form a solid mass which is cut once more. Each time the curd is cut, more whey is released.

As well as cutting the curds, the cheese maker may also heat them. This makes the curds compact and lose even more whey. Temperatures vary from about 34°C for cheeses like Caerphilly to 53°C for Parmigiano Reggiano to 90°C for Provolone. Herbs and spices may be added to the curds at this stage.

Moulding, pressing and salting

The prepared curds are ladled into perforated moulds which may be made of wood, stainless steel, basket ware or cheesecloth and can be of any shape or size. The cheese may be left to firm naturally, or it may be lightly or heavily pressed. The harder a cheese is pressed, the firmer it will be.

All cheeses, except the softest of cream and cottage cheeses, are salted. The salt helps to slow down the activity of the starter culture and so controls the rate at which the cheese later ripens. Salt may be added to the milled curds, as in the case of Cheddar, or the formed cheese may be soaked in brine as with Emmental. Other cheeses, such as Taleggio and Livarot, are washed with brine-soaked cloth or, like Parmesan and Roquefort, have the salt rubbed on to the surface.

In addition to being salted, the cheese may be sprayed with mould-forming spores to form a bloomy white rind; or it may be washed with bacteria to give a reddish-coloured, strong-smelling rind; or it may be covered in ash to give a black coating on the rind.

Ripening

During the ripening process enzymes in the cheese slowly change its chemical composition and it starts to take on its

own special texture and flavour. Ripening takes place in carefully controlled maturing rooms. Temperatures are kept low to ensure that the beneficial organisms included in the starter culture grow at a steady rate. Humidity is kept at high levels to stop the surface of the cheese drying out.

The ripening period is different for each type of cheese. Soft cheeses ripen quite quickly, and may be ready to eat within a few weeks. Hard cheeses, on the other hand, may take one, two or even three years to reach full maturity.

Classifying cheese

Because cheeses are so many, and so varied, it is difficult to classify them without continually listing exceptions. An individual cheese may well belong to more than one classification. Here, however, are some general principles which may prove useful to bear in mind when choosing and buying cheese:

Texture
Cheeses may be very soft and spoonable, soft and spreadable, semi hard and sliceable or hard. The last may be firm and crumbly, firm and slightly rubbery or firm and dense.

Strength of flavour
Some cheeses naturally taste (and smell) stronger than others, but all cheeses tend to taste stronger as they age.

Rind
White mould or 'bloomy' rind is the result of penicillin mould growing on the cheese. It is seen on fast-ripening cheeses, which usually have a soft texture. Washed-rind cheeses have been washed with a liquid that encourages the growth of bacteria that gives a pinkish-orange colour to the rind and a very strong smell. Dry natural rinds are formed by curds at the edge of the cheese drying out. Moulds may also grow on the coarser cheeses.

Additional rinds may be added by the cheese maker and range from herbs or leaves to ash, wax or plastic.

Milk type
The fat content of the milk from different animals differs considerably. Cow's milk, for example, is relatively high in fat

OPPOSITE: THE MATURING ROOM
This is where the ripening process takes place, and mould grows on the rind. Some cheeses, for example Camembert, ripen from the rind inwards, the centre being the last to lose its chalkiness. The French call this chalky centre *l'ame* or the soul of the cheese. These cheeses look quite different when they are unwrapped at home as the packaging flattens the furry down of the mould growth.

and gives a fairly creamy texture and taste, whereas goat's milk cheeses tend to be drier and sharper.

Blue veining
These cheeses are made by injecting moulds into the pâte which turn blue or greenish blue on exposure to air. The veins will gradually spread throughout the cheese.

Vegetarian
These cheeses use a rennet substitute. Rennet is an extract from the lining of a calf's stomach and as such is an animal product. Certain types of thistles can be used instead of rennet, but more usually the substitute is a commercially-made enzyme that mimics the effect of rennet. Some of these are genetically modified.

Low fat cheese
The flavour of a cheese is in the fat content, so, by definition, low-fat cheese will have less flavour than normal cheese. Some low-fat cheeses have artificial flavours added to them to make up for the loss.

Cow, sheep or goat?
Cheeses come in so many sizes, textures and flavours that it is hardly worth trying to contrast the differences between cow, sheep or goat. More useful are the broad categories given above; for more information about different types of rind, see the glossary on page 11.

Sheep and goat cheese happened to be the first to be made in ancient times - cattle were not domesticated until later. As stated above, goat's cheeses tend to be drier and sharper than cow's or sheep's - but this is by no means always the case. Sheep's milk cheeses generally have a nutty flavour, and they range from soft and creamy to hard and crumbly, but so do cow's milk cheeses. We make it clear in the entries on each cheese in the main part of this book what type of milk it is made from.

Cheese and the seasons
One of the delights of eating cheeses is appreciating how they change from season to season. Summer milk is different from winter milk. Winter milk from cattle that have been reliant on hay makes quite sharp, even stark-tasting cheese. Summer milk from cattle that have grazed on warm pastures makes softer, richer, even floral-tasting cheese. Autumn milk cheeses are the richest of all because the cattle graze on the strong second growth of grass, which comes up after grazing or mowing. Perhaps the best-known autumn milk cheese is Vacherin Mont d'Or, which is available only between October and March.

OPPOSITE: SHEEP IN LOW PASTURE
Tough, hardy creatures, sheep can thrive in much less hospitable environments than cows can. Regions with high, rocky grazing - parts of Spain, southern France, Italy and Greece, for example - produce more cheese from sheep's milk than cow's.

FINE CHEESE TODAY

It is well known that France produces enough cheeses to serve a different one every day of the year. However, the other European countries featured in this book all have fine traditional cheeses, and increasing numbers of excellent new cheeses, which are made and sold in some quantity, both locally and internationally. Cheese has been less important in the New World, but here too interest is growing rapidly.

Trends

The world of fine cheese is a buoyant one and new cheeses regularly appear on the market. Some are the result of existing creameries developing new products to suit their particular customers. The range of flavoured and smoked cheese, for example, is on the increase (but they tend to be of poor quality). In recent years, too, there has been an upsurge of new cheese makers working in traditional ways to produce a wide variety of 'artisan' cheeses.

This trend was particularly noticeable in Britain in the 1980s. Sheep and goats were the preferred animals for milk: they are a little easier to manage than cows. Recent years have seen more and more new British cheeses on the market.

In fact, there is a new sense of excitement in the world of cheese as communication grows between cheese makers in different countries and as they travel abroad in order to gain new perspectives. Events such as the bi-annual *Salone del Gusto* and International Cheese Festival run by the Slow Food Association bring together enthusiasts from all over the world.

New labelling

Certain cheese names, such as Stilton and Parmigiano Reggiano, have had nationally and sometimes internationally agreed protection for many years. In France the *Appellation d'Origine Controlée* system was set up in 1935, and applied first to wine and then to cheese. Eventually, 37 French cheeses gained the right to use the AOC symbol on their labels. Today, a new Europe-wide Protected Designation of Origin

OPPOSITE: LEADING CHEESEMONGER **Paxton & Whitfield, founded in 1742, is one of the great specialist cheese shops, with four branches in Britain. It concentrates on quality (Winston Churchill once observed: "A gentleman only buys his cheese at Paxton & Whitfield"), selling cheeses from the best traditional artisan makers in Britain and Europe. Cheese lovers visiting London should not leave without dropping in at the famous Paxton & Whitfield shop at 93 Jermyn Street, W1.**

(PDO) system is replacing the AOC arrangement and applies to specific cheeses across the European Union.

More outlets for cheese

Not only are there more and more cheeses on offer, but there are also increasing numbers of retail outlets for fine cheese. Equally important in this change has been the addition of cheese counters to many farm shops and farmers' markets.

Supermarkets have had a less important role in the change, as they concentrate mainly on factory-made cheese.

However, things are changing, and in some European countries the better supermarkets are widening the range of cheese on offer and some even stock locally-produced cheeses.

ABOVE: LOCAL CHEESEMAKER'S COUNTER
Cheese retailing is on the increase, but it is still tough for independents to compete with supermarkets: in fact, it's generally difficult for specialist cheese makers to find enough outlets for their cheeses without supplying supermarkets.

CHEESE AND HEALTH

Cheese contains protein, fatty acids (both saturated and unsaturated) and water. It also contains Vitamin A, small quantities of Vitamins B, D and E, plenty of calcium, and some other minerals such as phosphorous. Sodium is added, in varying quantities, in the form of salt.

Fat

The fat content of cheese is around 25 per cent, but recent research suggests that it is not all absorbed into the body. This is because cheese is so high in calcium. The fatty acids are carried through the body on the back of the calcium, which is at too high a level to be absorbed. Therefore, eating cheese is not thought to increase cholesterol levels. This is borne out by the fact that various epidemiological studies have indicated that there is no connection between the occurrence of cardiovascular disease and the consumption of cheese.

The fat content of cheese is usually worked out on the basis of dry weight and does not take into the account the water that is present in the cheese. Thus the figure for 45 per cent fat given on a box of Camembert, for example, is measured after all the water has been removed. It is more correctly referred to as 'in dry matter' (IDM) in the U.S.A. or 'matière grasse' (m.g.) in Europe. As a general rule of thumb, the actual fat content of a cheese labelled 45 per cent IDM or m.g. is about half that amount or 22 per cent.

Safe

Not only is cheese healthy, it is also safe. It carries a very low risk of food poisoning at 0.1 per cent compared with poultry and eggs at 33 per cent, salads, fruit and vegetables at 11 per cent and even water at 2.7 per cent.

Some people restrict how much cheese they eat, not only because they are concerned about their cholesterol levels, but because they believe, perhaps unnecessarily, that they have an intolerance to lactose. Most of the lactose in milk is removed during the manufacture of cheese. As a result, most ripened cheeses have lost 95 per cent of the lactose that was present in the whole milk from which they were made.

LEFT: Surprise 'cheesecake'

LOOKING AFTER CHEESE

In an ideal world, we would buy enough cheese for our needs that day and buy again the next. Cheese is best kept as a whole and specialist cheese shops look after their cheeses so that they are in peak condition when sold. However, it is not always practical to buy on the day of consumption and you may need to store cheese for a while.

Storing cheese

Most cheeses are best stored between 8°C and 15°C. Extremes of temperature should be avoided. If the cheese is too cold, it will gradually dry up and the texture and flavour will suffer, though it is possible to slow the maturation of a cheese by keeping it at a cooler temperature. If the temperature is too high, the cheese it will look oily and start to ferment. Humidity is also important: a relative humidity above 80 per cent is best.

However, these conditions are difficult to achieve at home. Solutions include a cool cellar, cupboard or garage, a cheese bell or even a large cardboard box. Failing these, you may have to use the salad box or a sealed plastic container in the door of the fridge.

Correct wrapping can also help to ensure good storage conditions for cheese. The waxed paper used by many specialist cheesemongers is reasonably effective: it allows the cheese to breathe, but not to dry out too quickly. Kitchen foil can also work well. Unwrapped hard cheese stores well in a sealed plastic box that is a little too large for it. Do not put more than one cheese in the same wrapping or box: their flavours will mingle.

Cling film is useful for preserving cheeses, but avoid completely wrapping cheese in it. This makes the cheese sweat, encouraging the growth of moulds. In addition, the gases given off by the cheese can be absorbed back into the pâte, making it taste unpleasant. Do not use the old fashioned remedy of a damp cloth unless you can be sure of regularly sprinkling it with water.

OPPOSITE: NEUFCHÂTEL CHEESE IN WOODEN CHEESE BOX
If you don't eat the whole of a soft cheese at one time, cover the cut surface with cling film, leaving the rind free to breathe, and return it to its box for storage in a cool place or in the fridge. Perhaps the cheese best known for its boxes is Camembert. The box, dating from the 1890s, allows the cheese to breathe.

Serving cheese

Cheese is wonderfully versatile and can be served at any meal. In north-western Europe the tradition is to serve the cheese towards the end of the meal – before the dessert in France or after the dessert in Britain. In Scandinavia, The Netherlands and parts of northern Europe, cheese is often served at breakfast. In Spain and Greece it is often served as one of the dishes in *tapas* or *meze*. But wherever you are, a slice of cheese and a piece of bread make a great snack at any time of the day.

Remember that if you have been storing cheese it should always be returned to room temperature for an hour or two before serving. Hard cheeses can also be refreshed a little by scraping the cut surfaces lightly with a sharp knife to remove any dried or discoloured paste. Soft cheese can also be scraped to remove hard patches. Wash the knife between scrapes.

Cut your cheese correctly and you will get more out of it. Cut it in the wrong way and the last to be served may well get all the rind. Also, if you do not use all the cheese at a sitting it will store better if it has been cut correctly. See the caption on this page.

Bread and cheese
Bread and cheese is an ancient partnership. Rustic breads with a substantial crust are the ideal choice and, as with wine and cheese, the best combinations are often the local ones. In Germany, rye bread or pumpernickel are happy partners for a well-flavoured Berkäse or Limburger. In France, when cheese is eaten with bread, the choice is usually a sliced baguette or some walnut bread, but often cheese is served alone and eaten with a knife and fork.

Accompaniments
There are many traditional accompaniments for cheese. In Britain, grapes used to be popular. Now chutney, sweet pickles and fruit are the fashion. In Spain and Portugal a concentrated fruit jelly made from quince is served sliced with the cheese.

Presenting a cheese board
★ A few carefully chosen cheeses will complement each other far better than a

OPPOSITE:
HOW WOULD YOU CUT THESE CHEESES? The shape of a cheese usually suggests the best way to cut it. Small round cheeses such as Banon and small goat's cheeses should simply be served whole or cut in half. Larger, round or square cheeses such as Camembert or Pont l'Évêque are best cut (like a cake) into triangles. Pyramid and log-shaped cheeses should be sliced. Small and large drum-shaped cheeses should be cut into discs and then into wedges.

larger selection that has been haphazardly chosen.

* Five different types of cheese make an excellent 'universal' selection: a goat's cheese; a cheese with a bloomy white crust; a hard cheese; a washed-rind cheese and a blue cheese.

* On the other hand, a single, rich, creamy cheese such as Vacherin Mont d'Or or Epoisses can succeed all on its own. A small selection of goat's cheeses can follow fish very nicely; poultry contrasts well with medium-strength creamy cheeses; pasta with sheep's milk Pecorino-type cheeses; beef or game with washed-rind and blue cheeses; lamb with Gruyère and crumbly English cheeses; rich stews with sharp, crumbly cheeses; dishes with creamy or full-flavoured wine sauces with monastery-style cheeses.

* Offer a choice of cheeses from mild to strong: not everyone will share your taste.

* Do not serve cheeses that look similar in colour and texture.

* Ensure that the board is not too heavy or too large to pass round comfortably.

* Put more than one cheese knife on the board, especially if there are some very soft cheeses that might stick to the blade.

Cheese and wine

As is well known, cheese has an affinity with wine. (One reason for this could be the fact that they both begin as natural products that are then transformed by fermentation.) Traditionally, red wine is thought to be the best partner for cheese, but this is a very limiting approach. Sweet white wines can be excellent with fresh-tasting goat's or sheep's cheeses. The French have long advocated (sweet) Sauternes with blue-veined Roquefort and flinty Sancerre with local Loire goat's cheeses.

The maturity of the cheese and the wine's acidity and tannin levels are the key considerations when putting wine and cheese together. As a (very) general rule, wines with high acidity work well with salty cheeses. As a rule, wines that are very high in tannin do not mix well with cheese. However, both wine and cheese are changeable products and it's best to follow the specific guidance given cheese by cheese in the main part of this book. Even here, the advice cannot be definitive: don't be afraid to experiment and follow your instinct.

OPPOSITE: PARTNERS
Very often, cheese and wine partnerships are suggested by the regions from which the cheese comes. The crisp Sauvignon blanc wines of the upper Loire go very well with the small goat's cheeses which are so common in the region. Mature Barolo goes well with an aged Parmesan.

CHEESE ACCESSORIES

There is an art to cutting cheese and the right equipment makes all the difference. Specialist cheese knives come in all shapes and sizes. They usually have a cured blade with a serrated edge and a curved tip to pierce pieces of cut cheese.

Some cheeses demand special treatment because of their texture. The pâte of very soft cheeses tends to stick to a blade, so purpose-made knives with holes in the blades have been devised to deal with the problem. Matured Parmesan, with its hard but crumbly texture is never cut but gouged out with a special wedge-like tool.

Cheese is usually presented on a wooden cheese board, but there are other suitable bases. Marble makes a firm base for cutting, and is easy to clean. However, cheese left on marble for more than a few hours may go slimy at the point of contact, where it cannot breathe. By contrast, straw mats and wicker trays allow the cheese to breathe and look appealingly rustic; however, they are difficult to clean.

LEFT: CHEESE BELL
A selection of cheeses presented on a cheese board and protected from the air by a glass cheese bell. Other cheese bells are made of pottery or china and have attractive designs painted or printed on them.

OPPOSITE: PURPOSE-MADE CHEESE KNIFE
The most useful specialist cheese knife has large holes in the blade. This allows the knife to cut through soft cheeses without squashing the pâte and it will also deal well with crumbly cheeses.

CHEESE DIRECTORY

It's easy to identify the classic cheeses in well-known cheese producing countries such as France and Italy, and you'll find them in these pages together with exceptionally full information. Not so easy is to shed light on the less well known artisan cheeses from all over the continent, but-this has been our aim.

Cheese-producing giants, such as France, have been given due attention - in fact over 40 pages have been dedicated to the best that France offers - complemented by stunning photography.

However, our focus on artisan-style cheeses has led us to some gems from countries not traditionally seen as quality cheese producers. Spain, for example, better known in gastronomic circles for its up-and-coming wine industry, produces some really interesting cheeses that reflect its often-ignored diverse landscapes.

Finally, smaller (but no less important) sections throughout the book are dedicated to the more obscure cheeses - reindeer milk and egg cheese from Finland, excellent but 'basic' Quark from Germany or aged Gouda from The Netherlands - for example.

FRANCE

If Charles de Gaulle were alive today, he would be predicting anarchy in France. He once famously remarked: "How can you govern a country that has 246 kinds of cheese?" In fact, today, there are more than 750 different cheeses or varieties of cheeses.

Despite the rise of the super-markets, traditional artisan cheese making remains deeply ingrained in France's national identity, with (very often) an unusually close relationship between product and place. For example, small, quick-ripening cheeses are typically produced in lowland areas and valleys where the journey to market was short. While making large 'wheels' of cheese that can be stored and matured (sometimes for years) is a tradition of mountainous areas where imme-diate selling was impossible.

Perhaps surprisingly, the most popular cheese in France is nei-ther Brie nor Camembert, which are the best-known French cheeses elsewhere. It is Comté, with Roquefort a close second.

FRANCE

FACTS

Size
**25cm diameter,
4cm high**
Weight
2kg
Fat in dry matter
45-50 per cent
When eaten
all year
In the shops
all year
Use
cheeseboard
Region
Nord-Pas-de-Calais

ABBAYE DU MONT DES CATS

Trappist monks first produced this semi-hard, washed-rind cow's milk cheese for their own consumption in 1890, at Bailleul Abbey in northern France near Godewaersvelde, ('God's plain'). They followed the methods of the brothers at Port du Salut Abbey at Entrammes, who started making cheese in the early 1800s. Abbaye du Mont des Cats is now produced in a small independent dairy using milk from neighbouring farms. Its small holes are formed by the gas given off during proteolysis. Affinage takes one to two months, during which the cheese is washed with brine and *rocou*, a red plant dye. The cheese melts gradually in the mouth and has a subtle flavour. It is best partnered with Graves or farmhouse cider, though in Flanders it is eaten at breakfast with coffee.

FACTS

Size
**36cm diameter,
8-10cm high**
Weight
7.5kg
Fat in dry matter
50 per cent
When eaten
all year, but best in summer
In the shops
all year
Uses
cheeseboard; Bleu Fondu à la Poêle
Region
**Rhône-Alpes;
Franche-Comté**

BLEU DU HAUT-JURA (AOC)

When France claimed Dauphiné in 1349, some of its peasants emigrated to the Haut Jura, where, encouraged by the Bishop of Saint-Claude, they developed this blue-moulded cow's milk cheese. It was an innovation, as sheep and goat cheeses had previously dominated the region. Enriched by mountain grass and flowers, the milk is mixed with spores of *Penicillium glaucum*. The cheese matures for one month, during which air is introduced via stainless steel needles to encourage the mould. The fine yellowish rind is dusted with white mould, and the creamy white, almost crumbly pâte is suffused with greeny-blue veins. It has a distinctly nutty flavour. Also known as Bleu de Gex ande Bleu de Septmoncel.

ABONDANCE (AOC)

Compared with other hard mountain cheeses such as Beaufort (page 46), which can weigh up to 70kg, Abondance is a lightweight at between 7 and 12kg. It was created in the 5th Century by monks of the Abbaye Notre Dame d'Abondance in an Haute-Savoie valley of the same name. The monks perfected the cheese, and in 1381 the abbey was chosen to be the official supplier for the election of the Pope, dispatching 1,500 kg of it to Avignon. Three breeds of cattle provide the required rich, creamy milk: the eponymous Abondance, the Montbéliard and the Tarine. Some 40 per cent of annual production is *d'alpage fermier* (farm-produced at an alpine chalet): these cheeses bear a blue *casein* label.

How it's made

After cooking and two pressings, the cheese is removed from the mould and cooled. It is soaked in salted water for 12 hours and dried before maturing for 90 days or more. Every other day salt and *morge* are applied to the rind to make it crustier, and to prevent mould.

Enjoying the cheese

Before eating, remove the canvas-etched amber rind and the grey layer beneath it. The cheese has a pale yellow pâte, small even holes and a pliant, velvety texture. It is strongly aromatic, with a complex and distinctive taste, combining the flavours of fruit and nut and balancing bitter and sweet. Try it with nut bread and a light wine.

FACTS	
Size	Use
38-43cm diameter, 7-8cm high	**cheeseboard**
Weight	Region
7-12kg	**Rhône-Alpes**
Fat in dry matter	
48 per cent	
When eaten	
all year, but best in summer	
In the shops	
all year	

FRANCE

AISY CENDRÉ

The story of this artisanal, semi-soft, unpasteurized cow's milk cheese begins with Robert and Simone Berthaut, who founded a fromagerie in Burgundy in 1954 and set about reviving Epoisses de Bourgogne (see page 60), which was in danger of extinction. Two years later, the cheese was in production. Once happy with the quality, they started experimenting. They discovered that by burying a young Epoisses in ashes as it formed, the cheese developed some unique characteristics. The ash reduced the flow of oxygen in and out of the cheese, changing its texture and flavour.

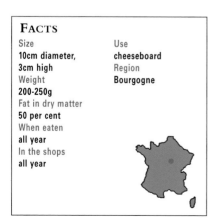

Facts	
Size	Use
10cm diameter,	**cheeseboard**
3cm high	Region
Weight	**Bourgogne**
200-250g	
Fat in dry matter	
50 per cent	
When eaten	
all year	
In the shops	
all year	

How it's made
The immature Epoisses, or other local variety, is placed in a bed of oak ash for a month or more. It gradually ripens. After it is removed, it is shaped into a disc. It is neither cooked nor pressed.

Enjoying the cheese
The layer of ash should be brushed off before serving. The heart is almost white and salty, with the chalky texture of plaster, and is surrounded by the creamier, earthier-tasting outer layer. Its strong flavour has hints of walnuts and hazelnuts, which is complemented by wine from the Hautes-Côte-de-Nuits villages.

BANON À LA FEUILLE

This soft cheese, originally made from goat's or cow's milk, or a combination of the two, is said to have its origins in Roman times. Recent production is associated with a couple from the village of Puimichel near Banon in Provence, and it is now only made from goat's milk. Leaves from chestnut trees that thrive here make ready-made wrappers for the cheese. It is uncooked and unpressed, with a fat content of 45 per cent, which makes it creamy and unctuous. The soft, white pâte yellows on maturing.

How it's made
Affinage takes two weeks, then the cheese is dipped in *eau-de-vie* and aged in chestnut leaves that have been boiled in vinegar and water to soften and sterilize them. As it ripens, the cheese takes on the colour and woody smell of the wrapping.

Enjoying the cheese
Within a rind of natural mould, the pâte has a soft texture and a creamy taste, reminiscent at first of milk, but gradually overtaken by chestnut and *eau-de-vie*. Eat it in summer with a peppery rocket salad, dressed with nut oil or, as the local farmers do, scooping it up with a teaspoon and eating it with a cooled Côtes de Provence, Rhône or Vin de Cassis (red or white) or a glass of *marc*.

FACTS	
Size	**Uses**
6-7cm diameter, 2.5-3cm high	**cheeseboard; with a sweet-and-sour sauce**
Weight	**Region**
90-120g	**Provence**
Fat in dry matter	
45 per cent	
When eaten	
best in summer	
In the shops	
spring to autumn	

FRANCE

BEAUFORT (AOC)

Christened the 'Prince of Gruyères' by the famous gastronome Brillat-Savarin, this extraordinary, large, hard mountain cheese is made from the milk of Tarines cows, a robust, hardy breed originating in Indo-Asia. Documents suggest that the Romans ate Beaufort, which is named after a small town in the Savoie. During summer the cattle are grazed on a diet of lush grass and alpine flowers, high on the local mountains. In winter the cows are sheltered from the snow in sheds. There are three versions: Beaufort, Beaufort *d'été* (summer) and Beaufort *d'alpage* (made in mountain chalets).

How it's made

Beaufort is cooked and pressed and, during its first pressing, a band (the *cercle de Beaufort*) is placed around it and tightened, producing the distinctive concave shape in its hard yellow rind. At a temperature of 15ºC and a humidity of 92 per cent, affinage takes at least four months and one to two years for a mature cheese. As it matures, it is wiped and rubbed regularly with brine.

FACTS	
Size	Savoyarde; Soufflé
33-75cm diameter,	Region:
11-16cm high	Rhône-Alpes
Weight	
20-70kg	
Fat in dry matter	
48 per cent	
When eaten	
all year, but autumn	
for Beaufort *d'alpage*	
In the shops	
all year	
Uses	
cheeseboard; Fondue	
Savoyarde; Tarte	

Enjoying the cheese

The elastic, grainy pâte varies according to season: winter cheese is white, summer cheese pale yellow. When young, the cheese is mild and fruity; when mature, it has a nutty aroma and a stronger, more complex taste. The *d'alpage* variety is the most prized. Beaufort is often paired with Volnay, Chablis or a local golden-coloured wine of the Savagnin grape. Perfect for fondues.

BLEU D'AUVERGNE (AOC)

One man was responsible for the creation of one of France's most respected blue-veined cow's milk cheeses. In the 1850s Antoine Roussel was a farmer and cheese maker in the small market town of Laquille in the Auvergne. One day he noticed that some of his *fourme* cheeses - non-stirred, lightly pressed curds - had turned blue. He tasted them, liked what he tasted, and determined that all his cheese should be blue. He achieved this by culturing it with the blue mould that he saw growing on rye bread nearby, piercing holes so the air filtered through and the mould proliferated.

How it's made
There are two sizes, both with a flat cylinder shape. A rectangular version is produced for export and pre-pack sale. A humid, well-ventilated cellar is used for ripening, the penicillin spores developing after three weeks. Affinage takes two to four weeks, depending on size.

Enjoying the cheese
Sticky, moist, crumbly, with an even spread of veins and a natural rind, Bleu d'Auvergne is a delicious partner for chicory, ruts, raw mushrooms and slices of pear or apple. It's also good in soufflés, on pasta and in salads. Compatible wines include: a red Côtes du Rhône or Madiran; a mellow white Jurançon; or a Sauternes. Banon, Epoisses and Puant de Lille are all cheeses that are sufficiently robust in taste to stand up to Bleu d'Auvergne on the cheeseboard.

FACTS	
Size	all year
Large:	Uses
20cm diameter, 8-10cm high	cheeseboard; salads; sauces; soufflés
Small:	Region
10cm diameter, height varies	**Auvergne; Midi-Pyrénées; Limousin; Languedoc-Roussillon**
Weight	
Large: **2.3-3kg**	
Small: **350g-1kg**	
Fat in dry matter	
50 per cent	
When eaten	
all year	
In the shops	

FRANCE

BLEU DES CAUSSES (AOC)

A milder cow's-milk relation of Roquefort (page 76), this flat, cylindrical cheese is named after Les Causses in the Rouergue where it is made: barren limestone country pitted with caves where the cheeses are matured. Natural chimneys (*fleurines*) allow cool moist air to pass through, carrying mould spores that promote the blue veins. Whilst Roquefort is made with sheep's milk, this cheese was originally produced with sheep's and cow's milk. The latter was more plentiful and less expensive, so began to be used exclusively, and Bleu des Causses became known as 'the poor man's Roquefort'. In spite of a meagre diet of wild aromatic plants, the cows are prodigious milkers.

How it's made
Uncooked and unpressed, the cheese ripens in the caves for 70 days to six months, taking on a robust, lively flavour. The damp breeze that blows through the caves imparts not just the mould, but also scents of the area.

FACTS	
Size	sauces
20cm diameter,	Region
8-10cm high	**Midi-Pyrénées;**
Weight	**Languedoc-Roussillon**
2.3-3kg	
Fat in dry matter	
45 per cent	
When eaten	
all year	
In the shops	
all year	
Uses	
cheeseboard; salads;	

Enjoying the cheese
Beneath a sticky natural rind of orange and grey moulds, Bleu des Causses has a moist, smooth, pale yellow pâte, if made in the summer (the winter cheese is whiter with a more pronounced flavour), liberally veined with blue mould. It is sweet and complex, with many of the characteristics of Bleu d'Auvergne (page 47), but is more assertive. Reds from Cahors, Fronton or Madiran are good partners, although a sweet white wine could also be interesting.

BRIE DE MEAUX (AOC)

Charlemagne liked this soft, unpasteurized cow's milk cheese so much that he ordered two batches a year. During the French Revolution Louis XVI apparently requested one last taste before his arrest. However it was Talleyrand who secured its fame in the 19th Century by organizing a competition to find the finest cheese produced by various nations. Brie de Meaux won. Nowadays, it is either *artisanal* or *industriel*. (See also Brie de Melun, page 50.)

How it's made
Each cheese requires a colossal 23 litres of milk, heated to a maximum of 37ºC during the renneting stage, but never cooked. It is cast into a perforated mould with a shovel called a *pelle à Brie* to drain in a humid atmosphere. The cheese is then treated with a dry salt, which is counter-balanced by the mild sweetness of the high quality milk. During affinage of at least four weeks in a cool cellar, the cheese is turned, the rind develops a velvety white *penicillium* mould, and the pâte turns a pale straw colour.

Enjoying the cheese
It is important to allow Brie to reach room temperature before eating. It smells faintly of mould, and the pâte is compact. The perfect cheese is plump, almost runny. It tastes creamy, with a subtle flavour of mushrooms. Over-young Brie tastes of cardboard; riper cheese has a hint of ammonia. Best served with a salad, crusty bread and Beaujolais or Burgundy.

FACTS	
Size	Region
36-37cm diameter, 3-3.5cm high	**Île-de-France; Champagne**
Weight	
2.5-3kg	
Fat in dry matter	
45 per cent	
When eaten	
all year	
In the shops	
all year	
Use	
cheeseboard	

FRANCE

BRIE DE MELUN (AOC)

Nicknamed the 'little brother' of Brie de Meaux, this less common *artisanal* version of the 'king of cheeses' is made in the same fertile region to the east of Paris. Before the railways, the fact that these cheeses were produced so close to the capital accounted for much of their success. Although the cheese is still traditionally made in Melun, AOC regulations now permit production in Seine-et-Marne, Aube and Yonne. Slightly smaller in diameter, but thicker than Brie de Meaux, Brie de Melun has a mustier aroma, and a stronger, saltier and more vigorous flavour due to slightly different production.

How it's made
The same way as Brie de Meaux (page 49), with one essential difference: whilst rennet is used to coagulate Meaux, Melun is curdled with lactic acid bacteria, taking at least 18 hours. It is also matured for longer than Meaux, seven to ten weeks. The cheese is kept on a straw mat on a wooden shelf in a cool cellar, under the eye of the *affineur*, who turns it twice a week and decides when it is ripe. The white rind is impregnated with a reddish yellow, wild mould and the pâte is an even ivory colour.

Enjoying the cheese
A perfectly ripe cheese has a rich, creamy texture and a robust, fruity aromatic flavour, with a slightly salty finish. It is delicious with a warm, freshly baked French country loaf and a full red Burgundy or Rhône.

FACTS	
Size	Region
27-28cm diameter, 3.5-4cm high	**Île-de-France; Champagne**
Weight	
1.5-1.8kg	
Fat in dry matter	
45 per cent	
When eaten	
best in summer, autumn and winter	
In the shops	
all year	
Uses	
cheeseboard	

BRIN D'AMOUR

This relative newcomer and perhaps most romantically named of all cheeses - Brin d'Amour translates as 'little bit of love' - is a native of Corsica, where it is made by hand from raw ewe's milk. It is unpressed and brick-shaped, with a natural rind that is rolled in a mixture of aromatic wild dried herbs, including rosemary, thyme, coriander seeds and savory. Maturation is for at least 30 days, after which the ash-grey herbs form a thick crust over a fine, whitish, curdy pâte. The subtle, fragrant herbs complement the slightly citrus taste. Closely related to Fleur du Maquis.

FACTS

Size
10-12cm square, 5-6cm high
Weight
600-700g
Fat in dry matter
45 per cent
When eaten
winter to summer
In the shops
winter to summer
Use
cheeseboard
Region
Haute-Corse

BROCCIU (AOC)

Another Corsican cheese, Brocciu, as it is known locally (or Broccio in France), is as old as the sheep and goats that graze the Maquis. It is made from the whey that is usually discarded after separation from the curds, and is similar to Ricotta. It is unique because it is the only whey cheese to have been granted AOC status (in 1988). Made from goat's or ewe's milk, it is ready to eat 48 hours after production, although it can mature for up to a month if it is drained and salted. Soft, milky and mild when fresh, sharper and spicier when ripened, it is sold all over Corsica in traditional woven baskets.

FACTS

Size
Varies
Weight
500g-1kg
Fat in dry matter
40-50 per cent
When eaten
fresh goat's cheese: spring to autumn; fresh ewe's cheese: winter to early summer; matured: all year
In the shops
fresh goat's cheese spring to autumn; fresh ewe's cheese: winter to early summer; matured: all year
Uses
cheeseboard; omelettes; pasta recipes; pastries and cakes
Region
Corse

FRANCE

Size
sold in 9cm-high cones
Weight
varies
Fat in dry matter
45 per cent
When eaten
cow's milk: all year;
ewe's milk: Dec to Jun
In the shops
cow's milk: all year;
ewe's milk: Dec to Jun
Uses
on fruit or desserts; in
puddings or sauces
Region
Provence-Alpes-Côtes
d'Azur

BROUSSE DU ROVE

Brousse derives from *brousser*, a Provençal word meaning to beat or stir. To make this cheese, the curd is beaten before being drained. Made from cow's or ewe's milk, it is an *artisanal* variety of *fromage frais*, which is made from milk coagulated by lactic fermentation rather than rennet. Brousse du Rove was once called *fromage frais de corne* because it was served in a sheep's horn; now it is sold in a plastic cone. High in moisture, it is milky, low key and sweet tasting. The scented herbs of Provence influence its flavour.

FACTS

Size
4-5cm diameter,
1-1.5cm high
Weight
30-40g
Fat in dry matter
45 per cent
When eaten
spring to autumn
In the shops
spring to autumn
Uses
cheeseboard; grilled or
baked and tossed in a
salad
Region
Midi-Pyrénées

CABÉCOU DE ROCAMADOUR (AOC)

In the old Southern French language, *langue d'Oc*, Cabécou means a small goat, and, not surprisingly, this centuries-old cheese - both farm and artisan versions - is made with raw goat's milk, formed into little disks. Its delicate flavour comes from the richness of this milk, produced on the pastures in the Rocamadour area where hawthorn, juniper and mulberry trees proliferate. Affinage takes up to a month. When fresh, the cheese is supple, creamy and mild, and melts on the palate with a sweet, nutty aftertaste. After a few weeks, the thin, wrinkled, whitish rind develops spots of blue mould, and the pâte develops a stronger, nuttier flavour.

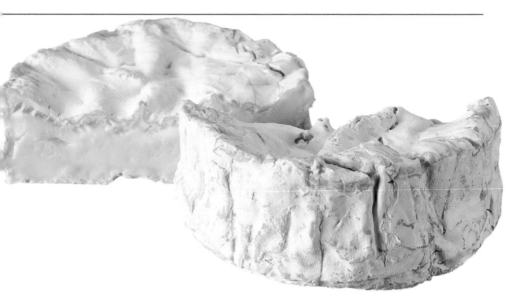

CAMEMBERT DE NORMANDIE (AOC)

Although Camembert is relatively young, it accounts for perhaps 20 per cent of all production in France. Its creator is said to be Marie Harel, a Normandy farmer's wife, who made a dry, yellow-brown cheese for her family in the late 18th Century from the milk of Normandie cows. During the French Revolution, the Harels sheltered a priest from the Brie region, who suggested ways to improve it. In 1855 her family presented Napoleon III with a piece, mentioning the name of the village it came from. He liked it, and from then on it was known as Camembert. Sales increased when a wooden box was designed, making transport easier.

How it's made

The cheese is made with raw cow's milk in *coopérative* and *industriel* versions. After warming, renneting and coagulation, the curd is cut and ladled into plastic moulds. Moulds are turned and covered overnight with a metal plate. Diluted *Penicillium candidium* is sprayed on the cheese; five days later dry salt is rubbed on the rind before a second spraying of mould. The cheese then rests and dries at 14ºC and 85 per cent humidity. After two weeks the typical white velvet mould forms.

Enjoying the cheese

Young Camembert is soft and crumbly becoming creamier as it matures. The best has a pale gold, pliant pâte and a subtle, mushroom taste. Best eaten with bread and accompanied by Sancerre, Burgundy, or Normandy cider.

FACTS	
Size	Use
10.5-11cm diameter, 3cm high	**cheeseboard**
Weight	Region
250g	**Normandie**
Fat in dry matter	
45 per cent	
When eaten	
all year, but best from spring to autumn	
In the shops	
all year	

FRANCE

CANTAL (AOC)

An ancient cheese that may date back to the Gauls, Cantal is from the mountainous Auvergne region, where winters are harsh, but the summer pastures remarkably fertile. A pressed cow's milk cheese, it is produced in a large cylinders. The original cylindrical wooden mould for the curd was called '*le formage*', from which the French word for cheese, '*fromage*', derives. The cheese was made large, so that the farmer's family didn't run out of food in winter. There are two types of Cantal: *fermier*, produced in summer chalets using raw milk; and *laitier* made all year with pasteurized milk from local farms.

How it's made
Milk is heated to 32°C and curdled with rennet. The curd is cut into small pieces, the whey drawn off, then pressed and sliced several times. The resulting *tome* is ground and salted before being moulded, and matured for one to six months or more at 10°C and 90 per cent humidity. Two smaller versions are made: one of about 20kg, and a Cantalet of about 10kg.

Enjoying the cheese
Cantal can be bought *jeune* (affinage of one to two months: very young); *entre-deux* (two to six months); and *vieux* (more than six months). Eat it with a Côte d'Auvergne or other local wine.

FACTS	
Size	Uses
36-42cm diameter, 35-40cm high	cheeseboard; grated on pasta or in soups; in sauces; Tuiles de Laguiole
Weight	
35-45kg	
Fat in dry matter	Region
45 per cent	Auvergne; Midi-Pyrénées
When eaten	
all year for *Laitier*; spring to autumn for *Fermier*	
In the shops	
all year for *Laitier*; spring to autumn for *Fermier*	

CHABICHOU DU POITOU (AOC)

When the Saracens migrated from Spain to France, they took their goats. When finally expelled from Poitiers in the 8th Century, they left them behind, plus their recipes for goat's milk cheese. From then on, goat breeding was established in the Poitou region and the nearby Loire Valley became France's centre of goat's milk cheese production. Chabichou (a dialect word from the Arabic for goat, '*chebli*') is cylindrical, and available in *fermier*, *coopérative* and *industriel* versions. When young, it has a rind of thin white mould, a dense, creamy pâte and a mild, quite sweet, nutty flavour with an underlying acidity. Once mature, the rind develops attractive blue-grey moulds, the pâte is harder and eventually crumbly, and the flavour more assertive.

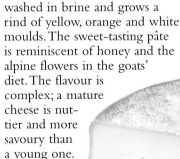

FACTS

Size
6cm diameter at base, 5cm at top, 6cm high
Weight
100-150g
Fat in dry matter
45 per cent minimum
When eaten
all year; *fermier*: spring to autumn
In the shops
all year; *fermier*: spring to autumn
Uses
cheeseboard; grilled on bread or salad
Region
Poitou-Charentes

CHEVROTIN DES ARAVIS (AOC)

A close relation of Reblochon, this raw goat's-milk washed-rind cheese is made in the Chaîne des Aravis in Savoie, and is different to the goat cheeses produced in the Loire Valley. It is pressed, and the fine, melting pâte is traced with small holes. Affinage takes two weeks to four months. The cheese is washed in brine and grows a rind of yellow, orange and white moulds. The sweet-tasting pâte is reminiscent of honey and the alpine flowers in the goats' diet. The flavour is complex; a mature cheese is nuttier and more savoury than a young one.

FACTS

Size
9-12cm diameter, 4cm high
Weight
250-350g
Fat in dry matter
45 per cent
When eaten
autumn to winter
In the shops
autumn to winter
Use
cheeseboard
Region
Rhône-Alpes

CROTTIN DE CHAVIGNOL (AOC)

Chavignol is a village near Sancerre; this cheese was made as 'fast food' for workers during the wine harvest. *Crottin* means 'horse droppings', and describes the look of the mature cheese. Made from the milk of thick-coated mountain goats, it is unusual for being enjoyable at various stages of maturity. Its appearance, texture and taste vary enormously as it matures. A fresh Crottin weighs 140g; after five weeks it can halve in weight. Amazingly 16 million *artisanal, fermier* and *industriel* cheeses are made annually.

How it's made
The cheese is raw and unpressed. Coagulation is principally lactic. Affinage is at least ten days, normally two to four weeks, and can be up to four months. A cool, well-ventilated environment is essential.

Enjoying the cheese
A Crottin matured for two weeks has a creamy rind with faint blue and white moulds, a moist, light texture and fresh, salty taste. After a month, mould covers the rind, and the pâte smells pungent, tasting more robust and nutty. Subsequently the rind turns brown, then black, rough and pitted. The pâte grows brittle with a strong, 'goaty' flavour. Perfect grilled and served warm on a salad. Also excellent on the cheese-board, best eaten with Sancerre de Chavignol.

FACTS	
Size	salad
4-5cm diameter,	Region
3-4cm high	**Pays de la Loire;**
Weight	**Centre; Bourgogne**
60-110g	
Fat in dry matter	
45 per cent minimum	
When eaten	
all year, but best from	
spring to autumn	
In the shops	
all year	
Uses	
cheeseboard; chèvre	

CHAOURCE (AOC)

This soft cylindrical cow's milk cheese is named after a market town in Champagne. Produced since the 14th Century, it was a favourite of Marguerite de Bourgogne. Farmers sold it at the world-renowned Champagne fairs in Troyes: the tradition of drinking Champagne with Chaource continues today. Previously only available fresh or *demi-sec* (slightly dry): now ripe cheeses are popular, mature Chaource is also sold.

How it's made
Production is both *artisanal* and *industriel*. In *artisanal* dairies, unpasteurized cow's milk is used, coagulation is mainly lactic and the cheese is ladled by hand, keeping the curd mild and light. It is not pressed, and affinage is usually two weeks to a month, but can be two months if in a humid cellar. Quality cheese is made all year round, but it is best in April and May thanks to the lush new grass.

Enjoying the cheese
Young cheese has a fluffy covering of *Penicillium candidum*. The pâte has a grainy texture and slightly nutty taste. When ripe, reddish stripes develop on the rind, and the interior becomes creamy and melts in the mouth, becoming almost liquid with age. Eat with Chablis, Nuit Saint Georges, Sancerre or Champagne.

FACTS	
Size	In the shops
Small: 9cm diameter, 6-7cm high; large: 11-15cm diameter, 5-6cm high	all year
	Use
	cheeseboard
Weight	Region
Small: 250g; large: 450g	Champagne-Ardenne; Bourgogne
Fat in dry matter	
45 to 50 per cent	
When eaten	
all year, but best in summer and autumn	

FRANCE

COMTÉ (AOC)

The most popular cheese in France, but still little known internationally, Comté is one of only two Gruyère-style cheeses produced in France. Cooked, and pressed into a large wheel, it is made from the creamy milk of Montbéliard cattle, fed in rich mountain pastures. The milk is free from additives and the quality of the cheese is assessed by examining the holes, or 'eyes'. A long affinage at a low temperature will eliminate these.

How it's made
Historically the cowherds, who took their cattle up to summer grazing, lived in remote chalets. They pooled their milk and made immense cheeses requiring long maturation, so they would keep until the return to the valley. The villagers still operate co-operative dairies called *fruitières*. The cheese is matured for four to 12 months (closer to 18 for Vieux Comté) below 19ºC and a humidity of 92 per cent. The rind must be kept moist, wiped with salt or brine, then treated with *morge*.

Enjoying the cheese
The rind turns to a hard golden yellow then brown crust. The pâte is firm, but chewy. The flavour is sweet and piquant, but depends on the length of affinage and season of production. Excellent with dry white, light red or the local yellow wine (*vin jaune*).

FACTS	
Size	wiches; salads; hors
60-70cm diameter,	d'oeuvre
9-13cm high	Region
Weight	**Franche-Comte;**
35-40kg	**Rhône-Alpes;**
Fat in dry matter	**Bourgogne;**
45 per cent	**Champagne-Ardenne;**
When eaten	**Lorraine**
all year	
In the shops	
all year	
Uses	
cheeseboard; fondue;	
***gratins*; toasted sand-**	

COULOMMIERS (AOC)

Although Coulommiers probably predates Brie and is more likely to have inspired its production than been inspired by it, this cheese is often referred to as Brie's 'little brother' and shares many of its more famous relation's characteristics. Made from cow's milk, it is disc-shaped, with a white penicillin rind. Production still takes place around the town that gave the cheese its name in the Brie region of Île-de-France, and can be *fermier*, *artisanal* or *industriel*, although the industrial cheese lacks depth and subtlety.

How it's made
Similarly to Brie (pages 49 and 50). Whilst pasteurized cow's milk is used to make the *industriel* cheese, the *fermier* and *artisanal* varieties employ raw milk. A special two-piece stainless steel mould is used, consisting of two hoops, one inside the other. Being smaller than Brie, its affinage can be shorter. The *industriel* cheese matures for four weeks, whilst the raw-milk versions need eight.

Enjoying the cheese
Best eaten at room temperature. Beneath its bloomy rind (thicker and crustier, with patches of reddish colour as it matures), is a soft, straw-coloured pâte. Serve with crusty French bread, or with a *parfait* spoon, and try Pinot Noir, or any robust red Bordeaux or Burgundy.

FACTS

Size	Use
12.5-15cm diameter, 3-4cm high	**cheeseboard**
Weight	Region
400-500g	**Champagne-Ardenne; Bourgogne**
Fat in dry matter	
40 per cent minimum	
When eaten	
industriel: **all year;** *fermier*: **late summer**	
In the shops	
industriel: **all year;** *fermier*: **late summer**	

EPOISSES DE BOURGOGNE (AOC)

This extraordinary washed-rind cow's milk cheese was apparently a favourite of Napoleon. Its origins can be traced to L'Abbaye de Citeaux, where Cistercian monks invented it early in the 16th Century. It fell out of favour during the Second World War, and was in danger of dying out until Robert and Simone Berthaut founded their Fromagerie Berthaut in 1954, reintroducing production in 1956. Pungent and complex, it can be enjoyed at different stages of maturation, and many gourmets consider it to be one of the most interesting French cheeses.

How it's made

Most farmhouses around the village of Epoisses used to have drying rooms and ripening cellars. One to three times a week, each uncooked, unpressed cheese is washed by hand with water or brine, mixed with marc de Bourgogne. With each wash, the quantity of marc increases. Brushes are used to spread bacteria over the rind. Affinage takes at least 30 days, or 40 for a mature cheese.

Enjoying the cheese

The rind is sticky and varies in colour from ivory to orange-brown, depending on age. A fresh, month-old cheese is dense, moist and grainy, with a subtle yet acidic, yeasty tang. Ten days on, and the fine-textured pâte smells strong and spicy, with an intense alcoholic flavour. Serve with a fine Burgundy, *marc*, Sauternes or a spicy aromatic white wine.

FACTS	
Size	In the shops
Large: 16.5-19cm diameter, 3-4.5cm high; small: 9.5-11.5cm diameter, 3-4.5cm high	all year
	Uses
	cheeseboard; melted over leeks
Weight	Region
Large: 700g-1.1kg; small: 250-350g	Bourgogne; Champagne-Ardenne
Fat in dry matter	
50 per cent minimum	
When eaten	
all year	

FOURME D'AMBERT (AOC)

Easy to identify, Fourme d'Ambert is tall and cylindrical and its dry, grey natural rind has reddish spots. Made in the Auvergne since Roman times, the cow's milk used for this mild blue cheese comes from herds that graze, between winters, on meadows between 500 and 1,500 metres up in the Monts du Forez. The cheese used to be made on the spot in the *jasseries*, or summer farmhouses. It resembles its near cousin, Fourme de Montbrison: *fourme* derives from *forma*, the Latin for shape.

How it's made

The cheese occurs in *coopérative* and *artisanal* forms, but most production has migrated to the co-operatives of the Monts du Livrodois and the Forez plain. It is usually made with pasteurized milk, although smaller makers still use unpasteurized. The curd is seeded with *Penicillium roqueforti*, and keeps a fine, light texture because it is shaped without pressing or cooking. Hollow needles let in air to promote the blue mould, and the cheese matures for between one and five months in humid, ventilated cellars. During this time the cheeses are regularly brushed with salt or wiped with brine.

Enjoying the cheese

The rather unprepossessing outside of this cheese encloses a firm, creamy pâte with occasional streaks of blue mould. Made all the year round, it goes well with Sauternes, or with Côtes-du-Forez, a local red wine.

FACTS	
Size	Region
13cm diameter, 19cm high	**Rhône-Alps; Auvergne**
Weight	
2-2.5kg	
Fat in dry matter	
50 per cent minimum	
When eaten	
all year	
In the shops	
all year	
Use	
cheeseboard	

FRANCE

FACTS

Size
13cm square, 5-6cm high
Weight
700g-1kg
Fat in dry matter
45 per cent
When eaten
all year
In the shops
all year
Use
cheeseboard
Region
Nord-Pas-de-Calais

GRIS DE LILLE

This square, semi–soft cow's milk cheese is also known as Vieux Lille, Puant de Lille and Puant Macéré, and the last two give a clue to its character. Puant Macéré translates literally as stinking pickle, and its pungent, smell and vigorous, salty flavour will keep it off the boards of all but the most robust cheese lovers. It is a type of Maroilles (page 67), but is cured differently. At about three months, affinage is twice as long, and the cheese is washed repeatedly with brine or beer, which eradicates the rind. The sweaty pink-grey surface encloses a sticky, elastic interior. It is best eaten alone or to round off a cheese board, with Champagne or, as the locals do, with beer or black coffee.

FACTS

Size
10cm diameter, 4cm high
Weight
250g
Fat in dry matter
45-50 per cent
When eaten
all year
In the shops
all year
Use
cheeseboard
Region
Nord-Pas-de-Calais

L'AMI DU CHAMBERTIN

Offspring of Epoisses de Bourgogne (page 60), this *artisanal* cheese from Burgundy has a more rustic appearance, with its sticky, wrinkled, orange rind, washed during affinage of at least one month with a mixture of water and Marc de Bourgogne. The spirit hardens the rind, preserving the cheese whilst allowing it to breathe, so the interior remains delicate and luscious. It has a penetrating aroma but a mild, milky flavour with a bolder earthy aftertaste. The milk used in its production is strictly from farms around Chambertin in the northern Côtes d'Or. Local wines or *marc* make ideal companions.

LAGUIOLE (AOC)

Pliny the Elder mentioned this raw cow's milk cheese in the 1st century AD but its first known producer was a monastery on the Aubrac plateau 1,000 years later. The monks passed on their method, similar to Cantal (page 54) to the *buronniers* (cheese makers) who still make cheese in *burons* (mountain huts). Laguiole (pronounced laïyole) is named after a local village, and has a thick, dry, natural grey-orange rind that darkens with age. The hard, pale golden pâte is smooth and pliant, with a complex, aromatic taste and slightly sour overtones. It matures for at least four months at below 14°C, giving a cheese of great character.

LE LACANDOU (AOC)

This raw *brebis* takes its name from Laurent Lacan, the cheese maker, who created, produced and refined it for 20 years in Aveyron. However the cheese came close to extinction in the 1990s, but it was rescued by Sévérac-le-Château in 1999, which bought the Lacandou label and produces the cheese today using the same traditional *artisanal* methods. The ewes that provide the milk graze freely over the local mountainsides, and are fed no silage, which accounts for the slightly perfumed, woodland flavour. The cheese has a soft, uncooked, unpressed pâte and a natural, cream-coloured bloomy rind. Affinage is about three weeks. Try it with a glass of Marcillac.

LANGRES (AOC)

A relative of Epoisses de Bourgogne (page 60), Maroilles (page 67) and Munster (page 69), this cow's milk, washed-rind cheese was created in the 18th Century on the high Langres plateau in Champagne. It finally gained AOC status in 1991, becoming well known outside the region since then. Its feature is its shape: cylindrical or cone-shaped, with a 5 mm-deep indentation at the top called a *fontaine* or *cuvette*, that can be filled with Marc de Bourgogne, Cognac or Eau-de-Vie which may be flambéed.

How it's made
Langres has two sizes; traditional *artisanal* methods are still used for both. Affinage is at least 21 days for the larger (five to six weeks is the norm), and 15 days for the smaller. Affinage is in a very humid cellar, where it is washed regularly with brine coloured with *rocou*. The *fontaine* forms when the cheese is turned twice during draining: the whey moving through the curd makes the middle subside.

Enjoying the cheese
The rind is sticky, with a reddish orange colour, and a pungent bouquet. The pâte is firm but pliant, and melts in the mouth with a full, complex flavour. Slightly milder than Epoisses, but creamier and spicier. Serve with a full-bodied Burgundy, Marc or Champagne.

FACTS	
Size	Uses
large: 16-20cm diameter, 5-7cm high; small: 7.5-9cm diameter, 4-6cm high	cheeseboard; in salads; as a dip
Weight	Region
large: 800g minimum; small: 150g minimum	Champagne-Ardenne; Lorraine; Bourgogne
Fat in dry matter	
50 per cent minimum	
When eaten	
all year	
In the shops	
all year	

LE PETIT BAYARD

Laiterie du Col Bayard, a family business for three generations, was founded in 1935 by Franck Bernard. Le Petit
Bayard is an *artisanal* cheese produced by the dairy and
named after it. Made from unpasteurized cow's milk, it is
neither cooked nor pressed and matured for approximately
30 days. It has a natural mould rind and a firm pâte, pitted
with small and medium-sized holes, and suffused with green-
ish-blue veins. Delicious with bread and a red Côtes de
Provence.

FACTS

Size
**12-13cm diameter,
5cm high**
Weight
450g
Fat in dry matter
45 per cent
When eaten
all year
In the shops
all year
Use
cheeseboard
Region
**Provence-Alpes-Côte-
d'Azur**

LE PETIT PARDOU

Most mountain cheeses are made in large cylinders or gigantic wheels but Le Petit Pardou is an exception. One of the
smaller mountain cheeses, it is made from cow's milk in the
southwestern town of Laruns, famous throughout the region
for its annual cheese fair. Le Petit Pardou and its sheep's milk
equivalent, Tourmalet, are
artisanal cheeses. Round
in shape, uncooked and
pressed, Le Petit
Pardou has a hard, dry,
greyish-orange rind
and a semi-hard pâte,
with holes of different
sizes spread. Affinage
takes a month, and the
cheese has a robust,
pleasingly rustic taste
and earthy aroma.
Perfect with a glass of
red Madiran.

FACTS

Size
**10cm diameter,
7cm high**
Weight
600g
Fat in dry matter
50 per cent
When eaten
all year
In the shops
all year
Use
cheeseboard
Region
Aquitaine

FRANCE

LIVAROT (AOC)

One of Normandy's oldest cheeses, Livarot was established by the mid-12th Century, probably by monks who taught their technique to local farmers. Named after a small town in the Auge valley, its soubriquet, 'The Colonel', refers to the five bands of sedge leaves or rush that encircle and look something like a French Colonel's five stripes. It was also known as 'meat of the poor' for being a nutritious staple in the diets of 19th Century French labourers.

How it's made

There are *artisanal* and *industriel* versions. *Artisanal* uses raw milk – preferably a mixture of skimmed evening and whole morning. The cheese is matured for one to two months in warm, humid cellars, washed with water or light brine coloured with *rocou*, and turned repeatedly. The *rocou* smoothes and colours the rind. As well as the regular cheese, three smaller sizes are allowed by AOC regulations.

FACTS	
Size	Use
regular size 12cm	cheeseboard
diameter of mould,	Region
4-5cm high	Basse-Normandie
Weight	
regular size about	
500g	
Fat in dry matter	
40 per cent minimum	
When eaten	
all year	
In the shops	
all year	

Enjoying the cheese

Livarot's aroma is pungent, bold, and its flavour spicy. It needs at least ten minutes to breathe before serving. The texture is moist and supple; colour and taste vary according to season of production and affinage. Eat with crusty bread and a white wine such as Pinot Gris d'Alsace.

MAROILLES (AOC)

Monks of the Abbey of Maroilles near Avesnes invented this semi-soft, washed-rind, square cheese in the 10th Century. It was dubbed '*la merveille de maroilles*' (the marvel of Maroilles) and is the grandfather of all Trappist cheeses. The monks passed production to the local peasants, who had to convert their cow's milk into cheese on St John the Baptist's day (24th June), and to deliver it to the Abbey on St Rémy's day (1st October) setting affinage at three months. Kings François I and Charles V are said to have been devotees.

How it's made

The cheese is not cooked or pressed, and, once in the moulds, is turned regularly and salted. It is transferred to wicker trays in a ventilated room called a *haloir*, where it gains blue penicillin mould. This is brushed away, the cheese washed with light brine, then aged in a humid cellar for one to three months. Three smaller sizes are made: *Sorbais*, *Mignon* and *Quart*.

Enjoying the cheese

Turning and washing eradicates the white mould and encourages the bacteria that forms its distinctive rind. It has a strong aroma of fermenting fruit, and a springy, oily pâte with a tangy taste. Partner it with Gewürztraminer.

FACTS	
Size	Region
Sorbais 12.5-13cm square, 6cm high	Nord-Pas-de-Calais; Picardie
Weight	
700g	
Fat in dry matter	
45 per cent minimum	
When eaten	
all year	
In the shops	
all year	
Uses	
cheeseboard; *Goyère*	

FRANCE

MIMOLETTE FRANÇAISE

Mimolette comes from *mi-mou*, meaning half-soft; because it used to be matured in Lille's *cave d'affinage* it is also known as Boule de Lille. This is a pasteurized cheese, made in a similar way to Edam (page 148). It may have originated in Holland and, when Colbert outlawed foreign cheese in the 17th Century, the Northern French started producing their own version. After six months' affinage, it is called *demi-étuvée* or *demi-vielle* (half old) and is firm, unctuous and vivid orange in colour from the plant dye, *rocou*. After one year, it is *vielle en étuvée* (old) and after two years, *très vielle* (very old), by which time the crust is brownish and pitted, and the pâte brittle and orange-brown with a salty, aromatic flavour.

MORBIER (AOC)

Originally made by herdsman in the Jura specially for the labourers who produced Comté, Morbier is a semi-soft, raw cow's milk cheese, which used to have a distinctive layer of edible, charcoal-grey ash running horizontally through the middle. Ash from the cheese-maker's fire was used to separate the evening from morning curds: this also protected the curds from insects overnight and prevented a rind from forming. Today, vegetable colouring is used instead. The cheese is uncooked but pressed, and usually requires two months to mature, after which it is rubbed with brine. Circular, with bulging sides, it has a moist, leathery rind, which varies from grey-brown to yellowy-orange. The ivory-coloured interior is springy, with a heady aroma and complex flavour of fruit and nuts. It is often melted, for example over potatoes in the local dish *Morbiflette*.

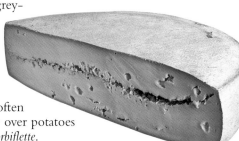

MUNSTER (AOC)

Irish Benedictine monks, who settled in the Vosges area of Alsace, began making Munster in the 12th century as a substitute for meat, which the order forbade, and to preserve their cow's milk. Munster comes from *monasterium*, the Latin for monastery. In Lorraine, to the west, the same cheese is known as Géromé. As with Maroilles (page 67), the monks taught local peasants to make the cheese, some of which was returned in lieu of rent. Production brought some prosperity to this deprived region.

How it's made
Farmers still use the generations-old methods, collecting the milk in the morning and evening, and salting the cheese by hand. It is first matured for a week, then put in a cool, humid cellar, on rye straw next to older Munsters, from which it acquires rind flora. It is rubbed with brine on alternate days. Affinage takes between one and three months. As well as *fermier* Munster, *coopérative* and *industriel* cheeses are produced.

Enjoying the cheese
This is one of the most pungent cheeses, but it smells stronger than it tastes. Inside the yellow to orange-red rind, the pâte is buttery with a robust, yeasty tang. Try to buy the raw milk version: pasteurization destroys its flowery perfume. It goes well with the local Gewürztraminer, Pinot Noir or Shiraz, or even a beer. Munster is eaten in Alsace with baked potatoes and finely chopped onions.

FACTS	
Size	mer to winter
13-19cm diameter,	Uses
2.4-8cm high;	cheeseboard;
Petit-Munster: 7-12cm	quiche;craclette;
diameter, 2-6cm high	omelette; grilling
Weight	Region
450g minimum;	Alsace; Lorraine;
Petit-Munster: 120g	Franche-Comté
minimum	
Fat in dry matter	
45 per cent minimum	
When eaten	
all year; *fermier*: sum-	
mer to winter	
In the shops	
all year; *fermier*: sum-	

NEUFCHÂTEL (AOC)

The first reference to this cousin of Camembert from Neufchâtel in Pays de Bray is in 1035 when Hugues I of Gournay gave it to the Abbey of Sigy as a tithe. Later, during the 100 Years' War, legend tells of local girls offering it to English soldiers, who thought it tasted like Heaven, and that the bloomy, white cheeses were angel wings. It only became popular in Paris 350 years later, after it was included in the *Almanach des Gourmands 1803-1812*.

How it's made
Cow's milk is used in the *fermier*, *artisanal* and *industriel* versions. There are six shapes: *carré* (square), *briquette* (small brick), *bonde* (small cylinder), *double bonde* (large cylinder), *coeur* (heart) and *grand-coeur* (large heart). The curds are not cut, but poured directly into cheesecloths and left, which gives it its grainy texture, unique among the velvety white-rind cheeses. Pieces of ripe Neufchâtel are then added to the curd. Affinage takes at least ten days, usually three weeks or more.

Enjoying the cheese
It smells and tastes of mushrooms, though some cheese lovers prefer it when the rind develops reddish pigmentation and an underlying flavour of ammonia. Excellent with crusty bread and red Beaujolais or Côtes du Rhône.

FACTS

Size	In the shops
various shapes: 4.5-5.8cm diameter, 5-14cm wide, 6.5-10.5cm long, 2.4-8cm high	pasteurized cheese: all year; unpasteurized cheese: summer to winter
Weight	Use
100-600g	cheeseboard
Fat in dry matter	Region
45 per cent minimum	Haute-Normandie; Picardie
When eaten	
pasteurized cheese: all year; unpasteurized cheese: summer to winter	

OSSAU-IRATY-BREBIS-PYRÉNÉES (AOC)

Probably the least known of all AOC cheeses, Ossau-Iraty is made from the raw milk of the distinctive black-faced Manech sheep. A traditional, semi-soft cheese usually in the shape of a wheel, it unites two Pyrenean regions: Ossau in the Béarn valley and Iraty in the Pays Basque. There are three main sizes: small (Petit-Ossau-Iraty-Brebis Pyrénées), intermediate (non-*fermier*) and large (*fermier*). Maturation is a minimum of 90 days (60 for the small cheese) at less than 12°C. The best cheese is made from June to September when the flocks are moved to high mountain pastures: its texture is supple and the flavour rich and mellow, with hints of nut, olive and fruit.

REBLOCHON (AOC)

Reblocher, means 'to pinch a cow's udder again'. In the 14th Century, Savoie landowners taxed farmers on the quantity of milk their cattle produced, so they would only partially milk their cows, reserving the second milking for themselves. Reblochon was - and is still - made with the second batch of milk, which is richer than the first. The milk of three local breeds is used: Abondance, Montbéliard and Tarine. Affinage takes two to four weeks, after which the rind varies from yellow to orange, with a sprinkling of white mould. The smooth, ivory interior has a fresh, delicate flavour, ideal with a white Vin de Savoie or fruity Beaujolais.

FRANCE

PICODON (AOC)

This quintessential French goat cheese comes mainly from the lower Rhône departments of Drôme and Ardèche. Picodon means 'spicy' in old *langue d'Oc*, and the aromatic scrub and tufted grass that grow in this hot dry region produce a sharp, tangy flavour. Milk is used from the hardy Chamoisée, Saanen or local goats.

How it's made
Whole milk is coagulated with a little rennet. From renneting, it is ripened for at least 12 days, often three to four weeks. Several variations of the cheese are available, for example in Ardèche, they are washed with spirits, dried, wrapped in vine and clematis leaves and sealed in earthenware pots to finish maturing. Some are marinated in olive oil flavoured with herbs.

Enjoying the cheese
Picodon resembles a small puck with a thin natural, mouldy rind that ranges in colour from pale ivory to soft white or blue-grey. It has a musty aroma. As it ripens, the compact pâte becomes brittle and crumbly and the spicy, sour flavour more pronounced. It is delicious grilled in salad. Try eating it with a glass of Saint Joseph white.

FACTS

Size	Uses
5-8cm diameter, 1-3cm high	cheeseboard; grilled in salad; fromage fort
Weight	Region
50-100g	Rhône-Alpes;
Fat in dry matter	Provence-Alpes-Côte
45 per cent minimum	d'Azur; Languedoc-
When eaten	Roussillon
co-operative cheese: all year; farm cheese: Mar to Apr, Sep to Dec	
In the shops	
co-operative cheese: all year; farm cheese: Mar to Apr, Sep to Dec	

PONT-L'EVÊQUE (AOC)

Normandy's oldest cheese is a creamy, washed-rind, cow's milk square, dating back to the 12th Century, when it was known as Angelot. Guillaume de Lorris sang its praises in the *Roman de la Rose (c.1237)*: *a good table always finishes with a dessert d'angelot*. In the 17th Century it took the name of the small town in the Pays d'Auge at the centre of its production; cheeses were soon being sold all over France.

How it's made
Three litres of milk make one 400g Pont-l'Evêque, and should be coagulated as quickly as possible after milking. The cheese is matured for six to eight weeks in a humid cellar on a straw mat, which leaves ridges on the rind. During affinage it is rinsed in brine, brushed and turned regularly to encourage the rind mould.

Enjoying the cheese
It has a firm, pale yellow body and an edible white-orange rind, which turns reddish-brown as it matures. Its aroma is grassy and its flavour mellow and savoury, with a sweet aftertaste. This is probably why Guillaume de Lorris chose to eat it as a last course. Traditionally, it is paired with fresh fruit (or even chocolate) and cider.

FACTS	
Size	Basse-Normandie;
10.5-11cm square, 3cm high	**Pays-de-la-Loire**
Weight	
140g minimum	
Fat in dry matter	
45 per cent minimum	
When eaten	
all year	
In the shops	
all year	
Use	
cheeseboard	
Region	
Haute-Normandie;	

POULIGNY-SAINT-PIERRE (AOC)

A traditional goat's milk cheese, Pouligny-Saint-Pierre stands out because of its distinctive shape, introduced in the 18th century apparently in imitation of its namesake town's belfry. Its nickname is 'the pyramid' or 'the Eiffel Tower'. It is made in the Brenne valley in Centre, where a benign microclimate nurtures the local vegetation to provide fertile grazing for the local goats and give a delicate perfume to their milk.

How it's made
The unique shape is made by ladling curd into pyramid-shaped moulds with holes. The curd drains for 24 to 36 hours before it is removed, salted and dried on willow trellises. Maturation is at least ten days, usually several weeks. After four weeks, the natural rind grows dry, with a striking blue mould. If affinage lasts longer, the rind becomes knobbly, its colour deepens and the beautiful mould spreads.

FACTS	
Size	Uses
6.5cm square base, 8-9cm high	**cheeseboard; grilled in salad**
Weight	Region
250g	**Centre**
Fat in dry matter	
45 per cent minimum	
When eaten	
***industriel*: all year; *fermier*: spring to autumn**	
In the shops	
***industriel*: all year; *fermier*: spring to autumn**	

Enjoying the cheese
Protected by the rind, the interior is very fine-textured, soft and white, with an aroma of goat and hay, and a complex taste, reminiscent of herbaceous plants and wine. It has a delicious sourness, which turns salty and then to a sweet nuttiness. White Sancerre makes the perfect partner.

RACLETTE

Originally from Valais in Switzerland, Raclette - or Fromage à Raclette as it's some-times called in France - is a cow's milk cheese, traditionally served cut in half, heated on a spit and melted over potatoes in their skins. The name comes from the French *racler*, meaning to scrape: the melted cheese is scraped off the block. The story goes that a 19th Century grape picker skewered a piece of cheese, which started to melt as he ate it beside a fire. Melting intensified the flavour and transformed an ordinary cheese into an extraordinary one.

How it's made
Made by both *artisanal* and *industriel* producers, it is uncooked and pressed, and must ripen for eight weeks or longer. Sometimes, it is mould-ed into a square, but it's usually a large wheel.

Enjoying the cheese
The thin rind is yellow-gold to pale brown and the ivory-yellow pâte is smooth, firm and open-textured which means it melts uniformly, without becoming greasy or liquid. The flavour is strong and nutty, with a hint of wine. Melted over potatoes, it should be served with pickled onions and a glass of Alpine-produced local Vin de Savoie.

> **FACTS**
>
> Size
> **28-36cm diameter or square, 5.5-7.5cm high**
> Weight
> **4.5-7kg**
> Fat in dry matter
> **45 per cent minimum**
> When eaten
> **all year**
> In the shops
> **all year**
> Uses
> **grilled over potatoes, steamed vegetables,**
> **meat and fish; in omelettes**
> Region
> **Alps**

FRANCE

ROQUEFORT (AOC)

The origins of arguably the world's greatest blue cheese supposedly lie with a lovesick shepherd who abandoned a picnic of bread and curdled ewe's milk at the mouth of a cave in the Causses to follow his girlfriend. Returning days later, he found the milk had turned to cheese and was covered in mould. The taste? Delicious, of course. Roquefort is still made from the raw milk of Lacaune sheep and matured in the Cambalou caves below the village of Roquefort-sur-Soulzon. Cheeses not ripened here are imitations.

How it's made

The *Penicillium roqueforti* culture, which used to grow naturally, is now induced by sprinkling a powdered form on the curds. During affinage of three to nine months, the cheese is pierced with a stainless-steel needle to encourage mould to grow throughout the pâte. The caves are cool (6–8ºC) and well ventilated due to the *fleurines* (page 48). When nearly ripe, the cheese is tightly wrapped in foil to reduce the rind.

Enjoying the cheese

Under a thin skin, the ripe cheese is dense, buttery and white with evenly distributed green-blue veins. Its flavour is unique and superbly complex, at once creamy, salty, sweet and tangy. It goes wonderfully with nuts, figs and Sauternes or port.

FACTS	
Size	salad dressings and in
19-20cm diameter or	salads
square, 8.5-10.5cm	Region
high	Midi-Pyrénées
Weight	
2.5-2.9kg	
Fat in dry matter	
52 per cent minimum	
When eaten	
all year	
In the shops	
all year	
Uses	
cheeseboard; sauces;	

SAINTE-MAURE DE TOURAINE (AOC)

During the Arab invasions of the Carolingian period, goat breeding was introduced to the Touraine region and its 'masterpiece', Sainte-Maure, was invented, although it didn't acquire its name for another millennium and production didn't take off seriously until after World War II. It is very distinctive because of the long straw that runs through its middle.

How it's made
The cheese is still produced according to traditional methods. Coagulation takes 24 hours and it is cast in a log shaped mould. The straw is inserted to prevent the delicate cheese from disintegrating and to keep it well ventilated. It is rolled in black wood ash and drained naturally before an affinage of at least ten days, but more often two to four weeks, in a cellar with a temperature of 10–15°C and a humidity of 90 per cent.

Enjoying the cheese
In the third week of maturation, blue-grey mould develops on the thin, smooth rind, and its ash coating affords a remarkable contrast with the white pâte. Young cheeses are moist, grainy and slightly citrus. When mature, they are smooth, creamy and aromatic, with a full, musty taste that balances flavours of salt and walnut. Partner it with a red Chinon or dry white Vouvray.

> **FACTS**
>
> Size
> **3-4cm diameter at one end, 4-5cm diameter at other end, 14-16cm long**
> Weight
> **250g**
> Fat in dry matter
> **45 per cent minimum**
> When eaten
> **all year; *fermier*: spring to autumn**
> In the shops
> **all year; *fermier*.**
>
> **spring to autumn**
> Uses
> **cheeseboard; grilled in salad**
> Region
> **Centre; Poitou-Charentes**

FRANCE

SAINT-MARCELLIN

Originally made with goat's milk, Saint-Marcellin is from the Dauphiné region, and has an impeccable pedigree: it was served to Louis XI in 1461. It wasn't well known at the time, as farmers produced most cheeses for their own consumption, only the surplus being sold at market. Nowadays raw cow's milk is mostly used. Usually round, with a natural, wrinkled rind, blotchy with white or blue mould, it matures for two to six weeks. When ripe, the soft beige pâte is deliciously creamy. It smells of nuts, and has a delicate, acidic, yeasty and fruity taste. To retain its texture and flavour, it must be protected from cold. Sometimes it is sealed, or kept in *marc*.

SAINT-NECTAIRE (AOC)

Louis XIV allegedly named this cheese in honour of Field Marshal Henri de La Ferte-Senneterre, who had introduced it to his table. It has been made for centuries in the mountainous Mont-Dore area of the Auvergne, where lush volcanic pastures provide grazing for Salers cows. Production is either dairy, using pasteurized milk, or farm, using unpasteurized (the latter has a distinctive green *casein* label). It is pressed, then matured for five to eight weeks on rye straw in old wine cellars, where it is turned, scraped and brine-washed. The cheese develops colourful rind moulds and a musty, farmyard aroma. The rich flavour is reminiscent of grass, walnuts, fruit and spices.

SALERS (AOC)

This hard raw cow's milk cheese from the mountains of
Cantal has been made for 2,000 years and, remarkably, production methods are said to remain unchanged. It is the only
exclusively farm-made AOC cheese and is only produced
strictly between mid-April and mid-November, when the
cows are out to pasture. Their diet is rich in aromatic plants,
such as gentian, anemone, arnica and liquorice, whose
flavours are transferred to the milk. The cheese is not
cooked, but pressed twice and
ground between pressings.
Affinage is between three and
18 months, and, as it ages,
Salers develops a pronounced
salty yet subtle, aro-
matic flavour.
Best with
light wines
such as
Beaujolais or
Val de Loire.

FACTS

Size
**38-48cm diameter
(before affinage),
30-40cm high**
Weight
35-50kg
Fat in dry matter
45 per cent minimum
When eaten
**all year (depending on
affinage)**
In the shops
**all year (depending on
affinage)**
Uses
**cheeseboard; in sauces;
grating; grilling**
Region
Auvergne

SOUMAINTRAIN

A round washed-rind cow's milk cheese from the Yonne area
of northern Burgundy, where Chablis is also made,
Soumaintrain is a (less extrovert) relative of Epoisses.
Although not AOC, it has become more widely available in
France since Fromagerie Berthaut, famous for producing
Epoisses (page 60), started to make it. Made with raw or pas-
teurized milk, uncooked and unpressed, it has a soft, creamy
pâte and is eaten young: affinage takes six to eight weeks.
The cheese is washed in brine, to which Marc is later added.
It has a moist orange rind, a powerful aroma and melt-in-
the-mouth texture. The flavour is rich, blending milky sweet-
ness with a spicy tang.

FACTS

Size
**10-13cm diameter,
3-4cm high**
Weight
350g
Fat in dry matter
45 per cent
When eaten
spring to autumn
In the shops
spring to autumn
Uses
**cheeseboard; fromage
fort**
Region
Bourgogne

FRANCE

SELLES-SUR-CHER (AOC)

Made for centuries by farmers for their families' consumption, this excellent cheese offered a practical way of utilizing goat's milk, and the craft of making it has been passed from generation to generation. Production became widespread during the 19th Century, but production was centred on Selles-sur-Cher in the lush country-side of the southern Loire. It is fine-textured and well-rounded. The ash covering below patches of blue-grey mould makes it easy to recognize.

How it's made
Approximately 1.3 litres of goat's milk make one cheese. Coagulation is mainly lactic, though a small quantity of rennet is added. It is coated with fine wood charcoal ash, which prevents the cheese from drying out and gives a good base for rind mould to develop. Ripening is for at least ten days, usually three weeks.

Enjoying the cheese
Beneath the rind, which the locals eat, the pâte is stark white, with a chalky, sticky texture at first, which softens and turns creamy as it melts in the mouth. It has a distinct aroma of goat and the taste, which is sweet and nutty, has tart salty overtones, which sharpen with age. Drink Pouilly Fumé with it.

FACTS	
Size	Uses
8cm diameter at base, 7cm diameter at top, 2-3cm high	cheeseboard; grilled in salad
Weight	Region
200g	Centre
Fat in dry matter	
45 per cent minimum	
When eaten	
all year; *fermier*: spring to autumn	
In the shops	
all year; *fermier*: spring to autumn	

TOMME DE SAVOIE

From the Latin *tomus*, meaning slice, *tomme* is a generic term and describes a small wheel of cheese, requiring little milk and produced on a small farm. *Tomme* is made throughout France, from cow's, goat's or sheep's milk, or a mixture. Tomme de Savoie, a cow's milk version, is the best known. Made with skimmed milk, it is uncooked, lightly pressed and matured for at least four weeks, during which the rind thickens and turns a rustic greyish-brown with red and yellow moulds. The aroma is musty and the ivory-coloured interior is sticky and speckled with small 'eyes'. It tastes mild and earthy, recalling grass, fruit and hazelnuts.

TRAPPE (VÉRITABLE)

The name translates as 'real Trappist', and not surprisingly this *artisanal*, washed-rind cheese is made in the Trappist abbey la Coudre near Laval in Mayenne. The abbey is not only home to the *fromagerie* but also to some 50 Cistercian nuns, who oversee production. The cheese is made with pasteurized cow's milk originating from Mayenne's abundant pastures, using the same methods as Port-du-Salut, whose monks passed on their recipe to the nuns. Uncooked and pressed, it has an affinage of three weeks in the abbey cellars, during which the nuns wash it regularly in brine. The finished cheese has semi-hard, pliant flesh, a faint smell of mould and a savoury, balanced flavour.

VACHERIN DU HAUT-DOUBS/MONT D'OR (AOC)

A relative newcomer, Vacherin du Haut-Doubs is a mere 200 years old. For decades the Swiss and the French argued about which country first made this ultra creamy, washed-rind cheese, now produced in the Massif du Mont d'Or close to the border. Recently both sides reached agreement: both can be called de Mont d'Or, but the unpasteurized French cheese is best described as Vacherin du Haut Doubs and the pasteurized Swiss version Vacherin Mont d'Or.

How it's made
The same 20 *fruitières* that make Comté in spring and summer produce French Vacherin between 15 August and 31 March, using the milk of the Montbéliard and Pie Rouge de l'Est cattle. The cheese is uncooked, lightly pressed, and shaped by a circular band of spruce bark. It is matured on a spruce board for three weeks, turned and rubbed with a brine-soaked cloth.

Enjoying the cheese
The golden rind, dusted with white mould, has soft folds. It has a subtle aroma of spruce which complements the other flavours of fruit, nut and milk. The yellow pâte is so runny the ideal way to eat it is with a teaspoon from its wooden box, with a Côtes du Jura or Champagne.

FACTS

Size
12-30cm diameter,
4-5cm high

Weight
various, between 500g
and 3kg

Fat in dry matter
45 per cent minimum

When eaten
autumn to late spring

In the shops
autumn to late spring

Use
cheeseboard

Region
Franche-Comté

VALENÇAY (AOC)

One of a number of goat's milk cheeses that have been made in Berry since the 8th century, Valençay was a perfect pyramid until - the story goes - Napoleon stopped at the Château de Valençay on his return from his crushing defeat in Egypt. When offered cheese in the shape of Egyptian pyramids, he furiously drew his sword and cut off their tops. Ever since, the pyramid has been square-topped.

How it's made
Uncooked curd is drained before and after being put in the mould. When solid enough, the cheese is removed and covered in salted charcoal ash. Affinage is in a well-ventilated room with 80 per cent humidity for three weeks. As the cheese matures, natural blue mould develops on the rind.

Enjoying the cheese
The farm-made cheeses are far superior to the mass-produced versions. The smooth, white, fine-grained interior has a mild goaty flavour, with a suggestion of hay and cherries. Young cheeses are fresh and citrus, but a nutty taste develops as they ripen. Valençay is excellent with rustic bread, roasted almonds or olives, and a white wine from the Loire: Quincy, Reuilly or Sancerre, for example.

FACTS	
Size	Region
6-7cm square base,	Centre
3.5-4cm square top,	
6-7cm high	
Weight	
200-250g	
Fat in dry matter	
45 per cent minimum	
When eaten	
spring to autumn	
In the shops	
spring to autumn	
Use	
cheeseboard	

ITALY

Cheese making in Italy has of course been been well documented since Roman times: Pliny the Elder described cheese making techniques, and cheese was in the rations of the Roman armies that conquered Europe. Cheese has always played a major part in Italian food culture, although two cheeses synonymous with Italy, Provolone and Mozzarella, may in fact have originated in ancient Persia.

Parmesan and Pecorino are also synonymous with Italy, and are rightly revered as flavour enhancers - for what they can add to a dish as a cooking ingredient. Outsiders are sometimes unaware that Italians also appreciate them in their own right for their robust flavours, eating a chunk with, for example, Parma ham and, say, a glass of Barolo.

ASIAGO (DOC)

Production of this popular cheese is limited to officially recognized areas in north-east Italy, with rich pastures. As with many rustic cheeses, it was first made centuries ago by nomadic shepherds to preserve their ewe's milk. Gradually they substituted cow's milk because of the higher yields. Asiago is still produced by artisan cheese makers, using traditional methods. The two varieties have very different characters: the older Asiago d'Allevo is matured, whilst the 20th Century Asiago Pressato is younger.

How it's made
Unpasteurized milk from one or two milkings is used for both cheeses: whole for Pressato and partially skimmed for d'Allevo. The curds are heated to a higher temperature for the mature cheese, whilst they are repeatedly cut, salted and turned for the fresh version. Both are dry-salted or brined, and moulded. Pressato is pressed and matured for 20 days; d'Allevo is unpressed and matured for five months to 2 years.

Enjoying the cheese
Pressato has a soft, pale straw-coloured pâte, with large eyes. It smells of yoghurt and tastes sweet and mild, with a slight piquancy. Darker, more compact, with smaller eyes, d'Allevo has a pronounced aroma, which intensifies with age, and a flavour of fruit and nuts.

FACTS

Size	**In the shops**
Pressato: 30-40cm diameter, 11-15cm cm high; d'Allevo: 30-36cm diameter, 9-12cm cm high	all year
	Uses
	cheeseboard; grated; shaved; in salads
	Region
Weight	Veneto
Pressato: 11-15kg; d'Allevo: 8-12kg	
Fat in dry matter	
Pressato: 46-48 per cent; d'Allevo: 42-44 per cent	
When eaten	
all year	

BRA (DOC)

Herdsmen began to make this semi-hard cheese from the milk of Piedmont cattle in the mountains around Cuneo in the late 14th Century. Once the cheese was ripe, they would bring it to market in Bra, where it got its name. Those who bought the cheese would mature it for longer in their own cellars, and either sell or eat it, sometimes as an ingredient in *pesto*. There are three varieties: Tenero (soft), Duro (hard) and d'Alpeggio (alpine).

How it's made
For the soft and hard cheeses, milk from two sessions is used, to which a little sheep's and goat's milk is added. The curd is broken twice before moulding, pressing and salting. The process for Bra d'Alpeggio is similar but more traditional. The cream skimmed from the evening milking rests overnight in copper containers and is skimmed again in the morning. Like Bra Duro, it is matured for three to six months. Bra Tenero has a 45-day affinage.

Enjoying the cheese
Whilst Bra Tenero is a delicate cheese, the two aged versions have a livelier, tangy flavour with a strong nuttiness. The colour – of both the compact pâte and thin rind – is darker and the texture heartier. A Piemontese wine is a splendid accompaniment.

FACTS	
Size 7-9cm diameter, 30-40 cm high	**Uses** cheeseboard; grated; shaved; melted; sauces; pesto; fondue
Weight 6-8kg	**Region** **Piemonte**
Fat in dry matter 45-50 per cent	
When eaten soft and hard: all year; alpine: Sep to Apr	
In the shops soft and hard: all year; alpine: Sep to Apr	

CACIOCAVALLO

Made from the 14th Century onwards, this is a *pasta filata* cheese, stretched and shaped by hand, in a similar way to Mozzarella (page 96) and Provolone (page 101). Caciocavallo means 'cheese on horseback', which probably refers to the traditional practice of tying two cheeses together and suspending them at either end of a pole to mature. People preferred the myth that it was once made with mare's milk.

How it's made
The cheese is hand-made from fresh, creamy cow's, or occasionally buffalo's milk. The curds are heated, drained and rested until they form a thick paste, which the cheese maker has to pull, stretch and knead, to eliminate air bubbles and form a sphere, then worked into a gourd-shape. The cheeses are salted twice and aged in pairs, slung together by rope, for three to 24 months.

FACTS

Size	shaved when aged;
15cm diameter,	grilled; melted; on
26-28cm high	pizza
Weight	Region
2-3kg	Molise; Campania;
Fat in dry matter	Puglia; Basilicata;
45-50 per cent	Calabria
When eaten	
all year	
In the shops	
all year	
Uses	
cheeseboard when	
young; grated or	

Enjoying the cheese
The rope leaves small grooves in the oily rind, which hides an almost white, smooth-textured young cheese, infused with the soft scents and flavours of the pasture's brushwood plants. As it matures, it dries and hardens; the texture becomes more granular – perfect for grating – and the flavour more vigorous. Try with a local red wine, perhaps Primitivo or Cirò.

CANESTRATO PUGLIESE (DOC)

A hard cylindrical cheese with straight sides and a slightly convex base, Canestrato Pugliese is made from whole raw sheep's milk, uncooked and matured for two to 12 months in caves. Its production centres on the province of Foggia and neighbouring Bari. Historically shepherds made the cheese in the early autumn when they were moving their sheep down the mountains as part of the animals' seasonal migration to lower pastures. Its name was borrowed from *canestri*, reed baskets made by local craftsmen, and used to mould the cheese. Using baskets instead of moulds produces a rough cheese with a rustic appearance.
Beneath its dark yellow crust, it has a dense, crumbly interior, ideal for grating, and a powerful taste.

FACTS

Size
**15-30cm diameter,
10-15cm high**
Weight
2-14kg
Fat in dry matter
45 per cent
When eaten
all year
In the shops
all year
Uses
**cheeseboard; grating;
grilling; melting**
Region
Puglia

CRESCENZA

A Stracchino cheese, Crescenza was traditionally made in early autumn, when the tired (*stracche*) cattle descended from their mountain pastures to the Lombardy plain. Surprisingly, when tired and hard at work, their milk is richer, though today production is year round. Made in squares or rectangles with whole milk from two milking sessions, it is ripened on cheesecloth-lined racks for eight to ten days. White and rindless, it is generally compact, creamy and moist, with a sweet, milky flavour, balanced by an underlying tartness, though the different regional versions vary. Some are rubbery and sharp tasting; the best are voluptuous and fresh.

FACTS

Size
**20cm square,
6cm high**
Weight
1-2kg
Fat in dry matter
48-51 per cent
When eaten
all year
In the shops
all year
Uses
**cheeseboard; on toast;
in sauces, omelettes or
ravioli; melted or grilled
on pasta or polenta**
Region
Lombardia

CASCIOTTA DI URBINO (DOC)

Michelangelo was such a fan of this semi-soft cheese, traditionally made with a combination of raw sheep's and cow's milk, that when he was painting the Sistine Chapel he requested a supply of it to be despatched to him in Rome. Casciotta describes a family of cheeses, established throughout central Italy when it was common to keep mixed herds and supply dictated which types of milk would be used. It is still only produced between April and September.

How it's made
Regulations state that 70 to 80 per cent of the milk must be ewe's (from Sarda, Apennica or Bruna breeds) and 20 to 30 per cent cow's. The milk is from the same day's milkings, and the curds are fed into cylindrical-shaped moulds made by local craftsmen. The cheese is pressed manually, salted and ripened for 15 to 30 days.

Enjoying the cheese
The yellowy-orange natural rind is thin and polished. The cheese has a milky aroma, soft, crumbly texture, and moist, gentle flavour that unfolds in subtle layers. It goes well with pears and a sturdy local wine such as Rosso Cònero.

FACTS	
Size 12-16cm diameter, 5-7cm high	sauces; pasta; gnocchi; risotto; panzerotti; pizza
Weight 800g-1.2kg	Region Le Marche
Fat in dry matter 45 per cent	
When eaten spring	
In the shops all year	
Uses cheeseboard; salads;	

CASTELMAGNO (DOC)

Named after the town that commemorates St Magnus, a Roman soldier allegedly martyred nearby, Castelmagno originated here in or before the 13th Century (a 1277 document records rent paid to the Marquis of Saluzzo in Castelmagno cheese). Annual production is only 50,000kg, making it one of Italy's rarest cheeses, and is limited to the high pastures between Castelmagno, Pradleves and Monterosso Grana. Demand fell in the mid-20th Century and it was only saved from extinction by DOC protection.

How it's made
Castelmagno is made entirely by hand from cow's milk, mixed with small quantities of sheep's or goat's milk or both. The milk from two sessions is partially skimmed. Over six days the curds are repeatedly pressed into cylindrical moulds then dry salted. The cheese is matured for two to six months in natural caves.

Enjoying the cheese
The pâte is yellowy-white when young, growing golden as it ages with piquant blue veins. Its distinctive flavour comes from evax, a grass that grows on the pastures. The texture is flaky and the rind hard and reddish-brown with grey moulds. A full-bodied wine, such as Barolo, will complement a mature cheese.

FACTS	
Size	fondue; sauces; pasta; risotto
15-20cm diameter,	
15-20cm high	Region
Weight	Piemonte
5-7kg	
Fat in dry matter	
45 per cent	
When eaten	
summer	
In the shops	
all year	
Uses	
cheeseboard; gnocchi;	

FIORE SARDO (DOC)

This hard whole ewe's milk cheese was probably made in Sardinia before the Roman conquest. Its popularity peaked during the 19th Century, when it was the only cheese to be exported from the island. It was favoured as an ingredient in the making of *pesto*, and sought after by merchants from Italy's principal ports. The name means 'Sardinian flower', which is apposite since its flavour is deliciously scented.

How it's made

Production is both traditional and industrial. It is made traditionally in mountain huts called *pinnette*, with a central open fire, above which the cheese rests on a reed shelf to acquire its distinctive smokiness. The curds are uncooked and moulded into cylindrical wheels. Brined and lightly smoked, the cheese is matured in a cool cellar for three to eight months, during which time the rind is rubbed with olive oil and sheep fat to promote affinage and inhibit moulds.

FACTS	
Size	shaved in salad; with
12-25cm diameter,	fruit
13-15cm high	Region
Weight	Sardegna
3.5kg	
Fat in dry matter	
40 per cent	
When eaten	
all year	
In the shops	
all year	
Uses	
cheeseboard; pesto;	

Enjoying the cheese

After three months, the dark yellow rind contains a firm whitish pâte with a sweet, herbal taste and a late piquancy that becomes sharper as the cheese ages. At seven months, the rind and the pâte have darkened, it has become rockier and the flavour beautifully balanced. Wines that go well with it include Sangiovese and Pinot Grigio.

FONTINA (DOC)

Proof that this partially cooked, semi-firm cow's milk cheese has been made in the Aosta Valley for centuries can be seen in depictions in the medieval frescoes that decorate the local castles, although there is no written mention of it until 1700. It is produced exclusively in the valley, enclosed by the Alps, where conditions are ideal for cheese making: the summers are dry and the pastures free of chemicals and filled with a wealth of mountain flowers and grasses, which flavour the cheese through the milk.

How it's made
Fontina is prepared with whole unpasteurized milk from Pezzata Rossa Valdostana cattle. The milk is fresh from the first milking of the day, and the cheese is made to a recipe passed down from one generation to the next. It is moulded, and aged, usually for three months, in natural caves, where it is turned every day, and salted and brushed on alternate days.

Enjoying the cheese
The finished cheese has a pale yellow interior, with a firm yet creamy and elastic texture and a smattering of tiny holes, encased in a thin, dense golden brown rind. The flavour is gentle, sweet and nutty, and it melts perfectly, so is the natural choice for an Italian fondue.

FACTS	
Size	fondue
30-45cm diameter,	Region
10cm high	Aosta
Weight	
8-18kg	
Fat in dry matter	
45 per cent	
When eaten	
all year	
In the shops	
all year	
Uses	
cheeseboard; melted;	

GORGONZOLA (DOC)

A Stracchino traditionally made in winter, Gorgonzola was created in the 9th Century and took its name from a local town, scene of an important cattle market. A host of stories have grown up around the development of its characteristic green-blue veins. One describes how a cheese maker left out some curds overnight. In the morning, they were covered in mould. Others suggest that it was invented in the Valsassina, where cool, damp caves offer ideal conditions for ripening.

How it's made
Most producers now use pasteurized whole cow's milk, to which they add *Penicillium* spores. They feed the curds into special sloping moulds, and after salting, mature the cheese in cellars - or in the Valsassina caves - for between 50 and 90 days. After three to four weeks, the cheese is pierced with needles to let in air and allow the mould to develop.

Enjoying the cheese
Gorgonzola is referred to as 'dolce' (sweet) or 'piccante' (piquant), the character determined by the length of affinage. Gorgonzola Dolce has a creamy, ivory-coloured body and a delicate flavour, with a sharpness concentrated in the veins. The pungent, dense, darker-coloured pâte of Gorgonzola Piccante is shot through with blue, and is crumblier with a stronger, spicier flavour. Pair either with fruit and Champagne or hearty red wines.

FACTS	
Size	bled in salads; melted
25-30cm diameter,	over potatoes; in dips
15-20cm high	Region
Weight	**Lombardia; Piemonte**
5-12kg	
Fat in dry matter	
48 per cent	
When eaten	
all year	
In the shops	
all year	
Uses	
cheeseboard; crum-	

GRANA PADANO (DOC)

Exploring ways to use their surplus cow's milk, the Cistercian monks of Chiaravalle Abbey in Lower Lombardy invented this cylindrical cooked cheese almost 1,000 years ago. Its long maturation, of nine to 24 months, meant that it could travel without spoiling and was sold at markets throughout the region. As its reputation spread during the 12th Century, other cheese makers took up production. It gained the name Grana because of its grainy texture. Made with unpasteurized part-skimmed milk, it has an oily rind, a fine, crumbly texture, deep yellow colour and subtle, perfumed taste. It becomes darker, harder and the flavour more penetrating with age. Similar to its better-known relation, Parmigiano Reggiano, a two-year-old Grana Padano is forceful and complex.

FACTS

Size
35-45cm diameter, 15-18cm high
Weight
24-40kg
Fat in dry matter
32 per cent
When eaten
all year
In the shops
all year
Uses
cheeseboard; on pasta or salads; melted; in sauces
Region
Lombardia; Piemonte; Emilia-Romagna; Veneto; Trentino-Alto Adige

MONTASIO (DOC)

Its name comes from the Montasio massif in Friuli, where it was created some 800 years ago by Moggio Abbey monks. Their original recipe used sheep's milk, but over the years cheese makers substituted cow's. Before the evening milking is added to the morning's, it is partially skimmed and the cream turned into marscapone. Three versions of Montasio are produced, with very different characters: fresh has a two to five-month affinage; partially aged, five to ten months; and aged, more than ten months. The fresh cheese is pale yellowy-white with a close, creamy texture, riddled with small holes, and a delicate fruity taste. The partially aged cheese is granular, with a more powerful fruity flavour, which intensifies in the fully aged version, as the interior grows craggier.

FACTS

Size
30-40cm diameter, 6-10cm high
Weight
5-9kg
Fat in dry matter
32-34 per cent
When eaten
all year
In the shops
all year
Uses
fresh: cheeseboard; aged: on pasta or salads; melted; sauces
Region
Friuli Venezia-Giulia; Veneto

MOZZARELLA DI BUFFALA

This delicious, mild-mannered, *pasta filata* cheese originated in Naples, where legend has it that a piece of curd accidentally fell into a pail of hot water at a cheese makers. This fortunate accident led to the creation of one of the world's best-loved cheeses. Nowadays, a lot of Mozzarella is produced from cows milk but it never achieves the finesse and delicate touch of the original buffalo milk cheese.

How it's made
Mozzarella can be made either by direct acidification of the milk to form the curds or by using the culture/rennet method. In both techniques, raw milk is pasteurized and coagulated to form curds. Once the curds reach a pH of 5.2 they are cut into small pieces, then mixed with hot water and 'spun' until long ropes of cheese form. When the proper consistency is reached, the curds are made into balls, which are then tossed into cold water to cool.

Enjoying the cheese
One of the key features of Mozzarella is its light, spongy texture (the cheese sold to make pizza is an inferior version). The taste is mild and delicate, with a slight sourness. The colour is usually white, although, depending on the animal's diet, it can have a yellowy tinge. Smoked versions are also available.

FACTS	
Size	Region
various sizes and shapes	**Campania; Lazio**
Weight	
various	
Fat in dry matter	
45 per cent	
When eaten	
all year	
In the shops	
all year	
Uses	
anti pasta; in salads; on pizza	

MURAZZANO (DOC)

This typical Alta Langa *robiola* (a family of Stracchino-style cheeses, robiola refers to the reddish rind moulds that develop as they age) has been in existence for many centuries: Pliny the Elder sang the praises of this type of cheese in his *Natural History*. Murazzano was originally made with whole ewe's milk, and is still by a handful of dairies, though most now supplement it with cow's milk. The proportion of cow's milk must not, however, exceed 40 per cent. Unlike most *robiola* cheeses, Murazzano is eaten fresh, after just four or five days of ripening, when it is soft, white and virtually rindless, with a dense pliant texture, and milky, subtly scented flavour. Also detectable is a suggestion of caramel, characteristic of sheep's milk cheese.

PECORINO ROMANO (DOC)

According to legend, the origins of Pecorino (the name for all pure sheep's milk cheese) lie in a shepherd's journey: before setting out, he filled his flask with sheep's milk, which was fermented by the motion as he travelled. The first written record is from the 1st Century AD, when agronomist Lucius Moderatus Columella offered some helpful hints on how to make it in his *De Re Rustica*. Painstaking dry salting produces a smooth, hard rind, and a maturation of five months to a year encourages the aromatic, tangy flavour, which sharpens with age. Traditionally made in Latium between November and June, production expanded into Sardinia when Roman cheese-makers could no longer satisfy demand.

ITALY

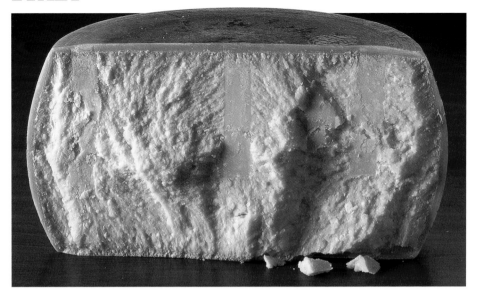

PARMIGIANO-REGGIANO (DOC)

For at least 800 years Parmesan has been made in Emilia-Romagna and Lombardy, regions to which production is still bound. Its nutritional value and special flavour lie in the cows' strictly-controlled natural diet, the consequent high quality of their milk, and the lengthy ageing process. By the 14th Century, makers were satisfied that they had created the perfect cheese. It has remained unchanged since and is now popular worldwide.

How it's made
Cheese masters persevere in the centuries-old artisan methods, using only 'milk, rennet, fire and art'. It is made in conical copper vats from partially skimmed evening milk, mixed with morning milk, and aged naturally for 18 months to four years. During this period, the drums must be inspected, brushed and turned continuously. To judge its internal consistency, a cheese-tester taps the drum with a percussion hammer.

Enjoying the cheese
Encased in an oily golden-yellow rind, on which the name is stencilled in small dots, the interior is straw-coloured, the shade dependent on the length of maturation, which also accounts for the formation of small white crystals. Although flaky and granular, it melts in the mouth with a wonderfully creaminess. The flavour is complex and well-developed, both salty and fruity: traditionally eaten with fruit.

FACTS	
Size	shaved on salads; in
50cm diameter,	sauces
35-45cm high	Region
Weight	Emilia-Romagna;
24-40kg	Lombardia
Fat in dry matter	
32 per cent	
When eaten	
all year	
In the shops	
all year	
Uses	
cheeseboard; grated	
on pasta or risotto;	

PECORINO SARDO (DOC)

Although Sardinia's tradition of sheep's milk cheese production stretches back centuries, Pecorino Sardo is a relatively new cheese (only receiving DOC protection in 1991), and less well-known than its cousins: Romano (page 97) and Toscana (page 100). Like all *pecorinos*, it is made with whole sheep's milk. Traditional, cylindrical and semi-cooked, it is sold in two versions: Dolce and Maturo. The first is aged between 20 and 60 days and has an elastic interior with small holes beneath a smooth, white rind. Whilst the flavour is delicate and fragrant, it has an acidic tang. The second is matured for four to 12 months, has a tough, brown rind and hard, cracked compact pâte. Its incomparable, rich spicy flavour finishes with a pronounced taste of caramel.

FACTS

Size
15-20cm diameter, 10cm high
Weight
2-4kg
Fat in dry matter
45 per cent
When eaten
all year
In the shops
all year
Uses
cheeseboard; grated or shaved on pasta or in salads; melted; in sauces
Region
Sardegna

PECORINO SICILIANO (DOC)

Sicily's oldest cheese was created more than 2,000 years ago: its name crops up in a list of cheeses compiled in the classical period of Ancient Greek civilization. Its invention was bound to the local agriculture: sheep's milk cheese production being the natural progression from the traditional sheep farming that is typical of mountainous islands such as Sardinia and Sicily. Cylindrical, uncooked and hard, it is made from whole milk, dry-salted two or three times, and matured over a period of four months. Not particularly well known, it is very similar to Italy's other regional *pecorinos*. The thin pale-to-deep yellow rind bears the patterns of the wicker baskets used as moulds. The yellowy-white interior has a pungent, but not disagreeable, aroma and a distinctive, penetrating flavour.

FACTS

Size
30-40cm diameter, 12-16cm high
Weight
5-10kg
Fat in dry matter
40 per cent
When eaten
all year
In the shops
all year
Uses
cheeseboard; grated or shaved on pasta or in salads; melted; in sauces
Region
Sicilia

PECORINO TOSCANA (DOC)

Sheep–rearing in Tuscany dates back to Etruscan times, and cheese making has its origins in the transhumance of the flocks, led by nomadic shepherds, who made fresh cheese as they journeyed. In the 15th Century it was called Cacio Marzolino (March cheese), because cheese making would always begin in March and continue throughout the spring. Production slowed down critically after World War II, but Sardinian shepherds crossed the sea to the rescue, grazing sheep in the neglected pastures, which coincided with the establishment of modern production plants. Pecorino is the only cheese from Tuscany that has been awarded the coveted DOP.

FACTS

Size	sauces
15-22cm diameter,	Region
12cm high	**Toscana**
Weight	
2-4kg	
Fat in dry matter	
35-40 per cent	
When eaten	
all year	
In the shops	
all year	
Uses	
cheeseboard; grated	
or shaved on pasta or	
in salads; melted; in	

How it's made

After the cheese has been pressed, it is some-times steamed to force out the whey. After it has been salted, a fresh cheese is aged in a cool dark place for at least 20 days, and a ripened one for four months. As the Toscana is smaller than most *pecorinos*, it matures more quickly.

Enjoying the cheese

A young Pecorino Toscana has a pliant texture and delicate, creamy, fragrant taste, with an underlying hint of walnuts and toffee. The aged cheese, on the other hand, is firmer with a more emphatic flavour of fruit and nuts, though it never approaches the sharpness or strength of Pecorino Romano (see page 97).

PROVOLONE VALPADANA (DOC)

The Romans were known to make a cheese similar to this *pasta filata* raw cow's milk variety from southern Italy, an older relative of Mozzarella. It comes in two versions: Dolce (sweet), which is young and mild, and Piccante (sharp), its matured, tangy counterpart. The term Provolone (which means large Provola, a typically stringy paste cheese) appeared in the 19th Century, when manufacture spread to northern Italy and it started to be produced in its now typical large size.

How it's made
The method is almost identical to that used to make Caciocavallo (page 88) and Mozzarella (page 96). Curds are stretched by hand until they are smooth and glossy, then worked into the desired shape - perhaps a sausage, ball, gourd, or pear. When finished, the cheese is brined, dried, tied with string and hung to cure for about three weeks for Provolone Dolce and two to 18 months for Provolone Piccante. The surface can be rubbed with oil to prevent cracking or mould.

Enjoying the cheese
Beneath its golden-brown rind, the firm pale-yellow body and subtle, smoky flavour of the Dolce version is replaced by a deeper colour and more emphatic taste in the Piccante variety. Excellent with olives and Prosciutto.

FACTS	
Size	**Uses**
various shapes;	cheeseboard; for
sausage: 30-40cm	grilling and melting;
diameter, 90cm-3m	on pizza
long; pear 12.5-30cm	**Region**
long	Lombardia
Weight	
200g-18kg	
Fat in dry matter	
50 per cent	
When eaten	
all year	
In the shops	
all year	

QUARTIROLO LOMBARDO

Herdsmen first made Quartirolo Lombardo 1,000 or more years ago in the Val Taleggio in the shadow of the Alps. A square, uncooked, soft cheese, it is similar to Taleggio in shape and taste (see page 105). It owes its name to the fact that it was made exclusively in September and October, when the cows ate *erba quartirola*, the fourth growth of lush new grass after the third and final mowing in Lombardy's valleys.

How it's made

Traditionally the skimmed evening milk would be mixed with fresh morning milk, a process still followed by some Alpine cheese makers, though nowadays most producers use full-cream milk. Salt is added to the curds as soon as they form, before they are fed into square moulds. Refrigerated storerooms have replaced the caves, where the cheese would mature for between five and 40 days. A thin layer of rind mould flourishes, protecting the interior and keeping it soft.

Enjoying the cheese

As the cheese matures, the wrinkled pale pink rind hardens and the reddish-grey moulds proliferate. The texture is springy with a crumbly, uneven centre, growing softer and denser with maturity. When young, it has a fresh citrus tang, which becomes mellow and fruity over time. Wines to accompany it include Lugana or Botticino.

FACTS

Size	salads; with cold meat or honey and dried fruit
18-22cm square, 5-6cm high	
Weight	Region
1.5-3.5kg	**Lombardia**
Fat in dry matter	
45-55 per cent	
When eaten	
all year	
In the shops	
all year	
Uses	
cheeseboard; in	

RAGUSANO (DOC)

An anomaly in Sicily, where most of the cheese is made from sheep's milk, this uncooked, matured *pasta filata* (where the curds are stretched or pulled) is produced with whole cow's milk. Named after the town of Ragusa, it is moulded into a rectangular block with rounded corners, a shape called *scaluni* ('step' in the Sicilian dialect), and is aged for three to 12 months in pairs, hung over poles: the technique used for maturing Caciocavallo (see page 88). Before it is sold, the cheese maker oils the smooth, dense rind, which turns from golden to brown with ripening. The pale compact pâte tastes gentle and pleasing with a satisfyingly savoury bite, which grows more pronounced and complex as it matures. Try Sicily's finest red wine, Nero d'Avola, with it.

FACTS

Size
15cm square
Weight
10-12kg
Fat in dry matter
45-55 per cent
When eaten
all year
In the shops
all year
Uses
cheeseboard; grilled
Region
Sicilia

ROBIOLA DI ROCCAVERANO (DOC)

This traditional uncooked Italian farmhouse cheese is made mostly from from semi-skimmed cow's milk (to a maximum of 85 per cent), blended with a smaller quantity of either sheep's or goat's milk, and is the only Italian cheese containing goat's milk to possess the DOP. Made in cylinders to be eaten fresh, it is ripened for only a few days or three weeks at the most. It has the thinnest ivory-coloured rind, which turns pale yellow with reddish moulds in a seasoned cheese. Beneath it, the body is milky white, tender, fine-textured and clean-tasting, though the flavour depends on whether the milk used is pasteurized or not. If it is, the taste is simultaneously sweet and sour. If not, it is slightly reminiscent of yeast.

FACTS

Size
**10-14cm diameter,
4-5cm high**
Weight
250-400g
Fat in dry matter
54 per cent
When eaten
all year
In the shops
all year
Uses
cheeseboard; for spreading; grilled; in salads; in sauces
Region
Piemonte

ITALY

RASCHERA (DOC)

The origins of the name have been the subject of debate, but the general consensus is that it comes from Lake Raschera beneath Mount Mongioie. The earliest documentary evidence dates back to 1400 in a contract, binding shepherds to pay rent to the squire of Pamparato in the form of cheese. There are two versions: Raschera, made on the plains, and Raschera d'Alpeggio, only produced in nine alpine towns and villages.

How it's made
The cow's milk is obtained from morning and evening milkings, semi-skimmed, and sometimes supplemented with sheep's or goat's milk, or both, to lend a spicier flavour. The curds are moulded, pressed and salted. Traditionally square-shaped for easy transport by mule, the mountain cheese is matured in a *sella* (a cool, humid room dug into the earth). The plains cheese is square or round, and ripened in a cellar. Affinage lasts three weeks to six months.

Enjoying the cheese
Encased in a thin even rind of russet-grey overlaid with yellow, the ivory pâte is pliable with small irregular eyes. The flavour, which is generally mild and aromatic with a suggestion of spiciness, changes subtly from one season to the next. Spring and summer cheeses are fresh, balancing sweetness and sharpness, whilst winter ones are lively and robust.

FACTS

Size
round: 35-40cm diameter, 7-9cm high;
square: 40cm sides, 12-15cm high

Weight
round: 5-8kg;
square: 7-10 kg

Fat in dry matter
45 per cent

When eaten
all year

In the shops
all year

Uses
cheeseboard; melted in risottos or over vegetables; diced in salads

Region
Piemonte

TALEGGIO (DOC)

Taleggio is a member of Northern Italy's Stracchino family of 'tired cow's milk' cheeses. Historically, cows would graze on the highland grasses during the summer months and then make the long walk down to the valleys in the autumn. The cows, tired from their long journey, would produce milk that was less watery, richer and more acidic than normal. It was on the menu for the banquet held in honour of the coronation of Pope Clement VI in 1344.

How it's made

After curdling the whole milk, the curd is crumbled and put into a rectangular block, where it ripens for around 35 days. The outside of the cheese is then washed either with water or brine. This gives the rind an orange or pinkish colour, and encourages *Brevibacterium linens*, which help to soften the cheese.

Enjoying the cheese

Although the aroma of a ripe Taleggio can only be described as putrid, it doesn't taste quite as potent as it smells. When accompanied with a glass of Nebbiolo or Syrah, its plump butter-fat texture – it turns runny as it ages – creates a delightful contrast with the subtle flavours of the wine. Deceptively strong and delicious when peaking, Taleggio offers a full and rich flavour that is hard to resist.

FACTS	
Size	grilling or melting; in
18-20cm sides,	salads or with fruit
4-7cm high	Region
Weight	**Lombardia**
1.7-2.2kg	
Fat in dry matter	
49 per cent	
When eaten	
all year	
In the shops	
all year	
Uses	
cheeseboard; for	

SPAIN

Spain, like France and Italy, has been producing certain cheeses in the same way for more than a thousand years. Its cheeses are also amazingly diverse - there are 40 different ones in the Basque region alone. Yet its fame as a 'cheese nation' is modest.

The Spanish might claim that this is due to its superb quality control system, which is as strict as it is successful. Each cheese must be made in a specific region and to certain criteria, making mass production almost impossible. This may make it difficult to find certain cheeses outside Spain, but quality is rarely compromised.

One famous Spanish cheese region is the Picos de Europa, where the lush uplands are ideal for cows and the limestone caverns perfect for bringing blue cheeses to pungent maturity. Cabrales is perhaps the best known of these strong mountain cheeses: usually ripened for three months, it is said to be preferred by the locals after six months, when it acquires a taste of maggots.

Afuega'l Pitu is another cheese with a kick - this time a fiery one. During the maturing process, cheese makers add fresh red chillies (perhaps to catch out any unsuspecting tourists).

SPAIN

AFUEGA'L PITU

Wedged between the Cantábrica mountains and the sea, Asturias is the richest cheese making region in Spain, and Afuega'l Pitu is one of its most ancient and popular cheeses. Fresh and creamy, it is made with unpasteurized cow's milk from an afternoon milking, and the curds are strained in a knotted cloth to give the cheese its conical or pumpkin shape. The name gives a clue to the taste: it means 'a fire in the gut'. Fresh red chilli is incorporated into it during production and rubbed into the rind as it ages, though the flavour is spicy and nutty, rather than fierce. The beige to deep orange rind has a coating of powdery white mould, and the cheese is excellent as a *tapa*, accompanied by bread and cider.

GARROTXA

A modern version of an old recipe, Garrotxa is a hard farmhouse cheese, produced by a small co-operative of goat farmers ('neo-rurals' dissatisfied with life in the city), who have applied their entrepreneurial talents to reviving a cheese produced centuries ago in this region. They have been remarkably successful. Made from pasteurized goat's milk, the cheese comes in a velvety disc, its rind covered in blue-grey moulds, with a stark white interior. Its aroma recalls the soil and the texture is smooth and buttery. The gentle, mellow flavour brings to mind nuts, herbs, and the fragrance of mimosa and fresh grass. When ripening is complete (after three weeks to three months), the rind is patted down with olive oil, which gives the cheese its distinctive fuzzy appearance.

CABRALES (DO)

For centuries, Spain's most famous blue cheese has been produced exclusively in Cabrales and three villages of the Peñamellera Alta region, on the northern spur of the Picos de Europa. It is produced by small family-run dairies, which jealously guard its origin and authenticity. Also known as Quesu Cabrales or Cabraliego, it is usually made with a mixture of unpasteurized cows', goats' and sheep's milk. Although produced year-round, the best cheeses are made during the spring and summer.

How it's made

Centuries-old production methods include the slow natural draining of the curds, kept deliberately soft and loose with plenty of air pockets, moulding and hand-salting. The cheese is turned and aired for several weeks, after which the slow maturing process is continued for two to four months in natural mountain caves, where conditions favour the *Penicillium* mould responsible for its characteristic blue-green veins.

Enjoying the cheese

Inside the foil wrapping that has replaced the traditional maple leaves, the cheese has a slightly sticky yellow rind with a pungent aroma and a compact interior pitted with holes and threaded with veins. Though energetic and tart, the flavour is not as strong as the smell. It goes well with salami and a full-bodied red wine or a sweet sherry such as Pedro Ximenez or sweet Oloroso.

FACTS	
Size	Region
20cm diameter, 7-15cm high	**Asturias**
Weight	
2-4kg	
Fat in dry matter	
50-55 per cent	
When eaten	
all year	
In the shops	
all year	
Uses	
cheeseboard; with honey	

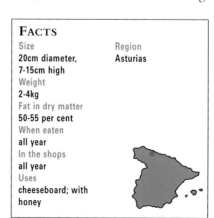

SPAIN

IDIAZÁBAL (DO)

FACTS

Size
10-30cm diameter, 8-12cm high
Weight
900g-3kg
Fat in dry matter
45 per cent
When eaten
all year
In the shops
all year
Uses
cheeseboard; for grilling and grating
Region
Basque; Navarra

Many years ago, Basque shepherds spent the spring and summer months high in the mountains above the village of Idiazábal in small rural huts called *txabolas*. There was little room to store and mature their hand-made raw sheep's milk cheeses so they would hang them in any available space until they returned to Idiazábal in the autumn, when an important farmers' market was held there. The cheese would absorb smoke from the shepherds' nightly wood fires. Although methods are still traditional, most production is now industrial and artisan makers are rare. The orange-brown rind bears the marks of the wood moulds used for draining, and the cheese inside is dense and firm. The natural smoking never overpowers the flavour, which emerges as fragrant and buttery.

MAHÓN (DO)

FACTS

Size
20cm square, 6-8cm high
Weight
1-4kg
Fat in dry matter
approx. 45 per cent
When eaten
all year
In the shops
all year
Uses
cheeseboard; grated on pasta
Region
Menorca

This pillow-shaped, washed-rind, artisan cheese from the Balearic island of Minorca was originally made with sheep's milk, but since the British briefly occupied the island in the 18th Century, accompanied by their Friesian cattle, cow's milk has been used. To form the shape, the curds are placed in a cloth, whose corners are knotted and twisted together. The cheese is immersed in brine and, after a month, the rind rubbed with a blend of oil, butter and paprika. The different varieties range from semi-cured (two months) to old (a year). The cheese tends to be dense and crumbly (granular when mature), with a fruity or nutty bouquet and buttery flavour overlaid with a salty tartness. It is traditionally eaten sprinkled with olive oil, black pepper and tarragon.

MANCHEGO (DO)

Invented by the Romans, Spain's most significant and famous sheep's milk cheese has a long historic and literary tradition. Its origins lie in La Mancha, Don Quixote's homeland, and Cervantes mentions it in his masterpiece. Made in two versions, unpasteurized farmhouse and pasteurized industrial, the cheese is flavoured by the perfumed shrubs and grasses that make up the diet of the hardy sheep of the region, and is now popular worldwide.

How it's made
The curds are shaped in moulds made of *esparto* grass, which leave a characteristic zigzag pattern along the side of the rind. The small wooden boards used to press the cheese for several hours also leave imprints of the wheatear pattern on its top and bottom. It can either be dry-salted or dipped in brine, and ripened for between two and ten months.

Enjoying the cheese
The yellow to brown rind is closed and waxy. Ranging in colour from ivory to pale yellow, the interior is firm, compact and slightly oily, with an uneven spread of small eyes. The flavour is very distinctive, deep and rounded but not too assertive (depending on how long it's matured), buttery and slightly spicy with hints of nuts and caramel on the finish. Choose a young red Valdepeñas or Rioja to accompany it.

FACTS	
Size	Region
20-22.5cm diameter, 10-12.5cm high	**La Mancha**
Weight	
2-3.5kg	
Fat in dry matter	
50-55 per cent	
When eaten	
all year	
In the shops	
all year	
Use	
cheeseboard; for grating or grilling	

SPAIN

PICÓN (DO)

FACTS

Size
**20cm diameter,
10cm high**
Weight
3kg
Fat in dry matter
55 per cent
When eaten
all year
In the shops
all year
Uses
**cheeseboard; with
honey**
Region
Cantabria

The early French pilgrims, who walked the Santiago de Compostella route, introduced this creamy blue cheese into Spain. The name comes from the vast mountain ranges that are home to the highest pastures and to more than 20 varieties of cheese. Closely related to Cabrales (see page 109), it is usually made from cows' milk, sometimes combined with a little sheep's and goats' milk depending on supply. It is ripened for two to three months in caves along the Cantabrian Sea, and wrapped in leaves, a combination that accounts for its unique autumnal saline flavour. Cylindrical in shape, it has moist, crumbly flesh with an emphatic aroma and blue-green veining. Creamier and mellower than Cabrales, it is often eaten with honey for breakfast.

QUESO IBORES (DO)

FACTS

Size
**11-15cm diameter,
5-9cm high**
Weight
650g-1.2kg
Fat in dry matter
45 per cent
When eaten
all year
In the shops
all year
Use
cheeseboard
Region
Extremadura

Produced in Extremadura since Roman times, this hard raw goat's milk cheese is simple and rustic, reflecting its native terrain. Snuggled up to the Portuguese border, Extremadura is not only the wildest, least developed region of Spain, it is also the most impoverished. During a two-month affinage, the rind of the cheese is rubbed with a mixture of olive oil and paprika, which gives it a deep red colour and the pâte beneath a piquancy and spicy aroma. In stark contrast to the rind, the pâte is milky white and creamy in texture, though it becomes harder and more compact as it matures. Older cheeses also have a more assertive flavour. Serve with fresh fruit or vegetables and a rosé from Navarre or white from Rias Baixas.

QUESO MAJORERO (DO)

Aficionados consider this hard, cylindrical cheese one of the best goat's milk varieties in Spain. It is sometimes called Queso Fuerteventura, after the Canary Island where it is produced, whose farming tradition stretches back 1,000 years. The principal factors that determine its high quality and aromatic flavour are the grazing, which - due to the hot dry climate - is not lush, but rich in fragrant herbs and plants, and the tough adaptable character of the Majorera goats, who produce a thick, creamy, scented milk.

How it's made

Unpasteurized milk is used (15 per cent of which may be Canarian sheep's milk), and the curds are pressed and moulded in a *cincho de palma* (palm and wood mould). The cheese is dry-salted and aired before ageing from eight to 60 days, when it is often rubbed with oil, paprika or *gofio* (toasted local flour) to keep it moist.

Enjoying the cheese

The rind bears the impression of the mould and is white in young cheeses, but turns brownish and abrasive in aged ones. The pâte is compact and sticky, with an even spread of holes and a tangy, buttery taste. There are underlying flavours of honey, almonds and wild herbs, and a peppery finish. Pair it with dry white wine or sweet sherry.

FACTS	
Size	pasta or vegetables
15-35cm diameter, 6-9cm high	Region
	Fuerteventura
Weight	
1-6kg	
Fat in dry matter	
52-55 per cent	
When eaten	
all year	
In the shops	
all year	
Use	
cheeseboard; for grilling; melted on	

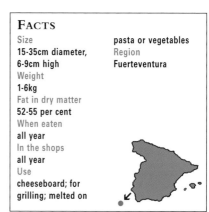

SPAIN

QUESO DE MURCIA (DO)

FACTS

Size
12-18cm diameter, 7-9cm high; small: 7-9cm diameter, 6-7cm high
Weight
1-2kg; small 400g
Fat in dry matter
45 per cent
When eaten
all year
In the shops
all year
Use
cheeseboard; in sauces when mature
Region
Murcia

In the arid mountains of Murcia, the goats graze on whatever they can find, mostly scrub and aromatic herbs. The dryness means that their milk production is low, but what they do produce is rich, wonderfully fragrant and perfect for cheese making. There are two versions of this artisan cheese: the original is fresh, uncooked, moulded and lightly pressed. Snow white and soft, it has a sophisticated flavour that balances the herbs with the acidity typical of goat's milk. As its shelf life is too short for export, a matured version was introduced. This cheese is soaked in local *doble pasta* wine for two to three days, and then ripened for 60 to 75 days. The wine turns the rind violet and the hard interior adopts its fruity piquancy.

TETILLA (DO)

FACTS

Size
9-15cm base diameter, 9-15cm high
Weight
500g-1.5kg
Fat in dry matter
45 per cent
When eaten
all year
In the shops
all year
Uses
cheeseboard; melted in sauces, sandwiches or over vegetables
Region
Galicia

The name defines the shape of Galicia's most famous and recognizable cheese: *tetilla* is the Spanish word for 'nipple', and the cheese is a flattened-pear shape, reminiscent of a breast, with a small nipple on top. Agriculture thrives in Galicia's humid maritime climate and rolling countryside, and the region produces the highest quota of cow's milk in Spain. The breed that produces the milk for Tetilla is Rubia Gallega, which are not prodigious milkers, but whose milk is of a superior quality. Not surprisingly there are Tetilla-makers in every corner of the region, industrial producers alongside small artisan farms. After a two to three week-maturation, it has a fine, yellow rind, smooth, pliable flesh and clean, buttery flavour. Pair it with Rioja or a dry sherry.

RONCAL (DO)

The first Spanish cheese to gain the coveted Denominación de Origen comes from the Roncal Valley in the northern region of Navarre, which borders France. Here shepherding is a way of life that dates back to 882 A.D. when King Sancho García bestowed grazing rights on the valley's inhabitants in appreciation of their bravery in fighting the Saracens. Cheese production evolved from the herding, and this variety is made with unpasteurized sheep's milk from the Lacha and Aragon breeds, both excellent milkers.

How it's made
The traditional hand-crafted method (an undocumented and jealously guarded secret) is still passed down verbally from one generation of cheese makers to the next, although some artisan producers have been transformed into industrial-sized dairies. We know that the curds are shaped into cylinders in beech wood moulds and pressed, and that the cheese is brined for 30 hours and aged for at least four months.

Enjoying the cheese
The rind is thick and normally the colour of straw or dark grey depending on the cheese's age. The compact, crumbly interior ranges from ivory white to amber and has no eyes. It emits an earthy aroma of straw and mushrooms, and the flavour is rounded, hearty and olivey with slightly tart overtones. Serve it with a red Navarran wine.

FACTS	
Size	or shaved on pasta or
15-20cm diameter,	in salads; melted; in
10 m high	sauces
Weight	Region
1-3kg	Navarra
Fat in dry matter	
45-50 per cent	
When eaten	
all year	
In the shops	
all year	
Uses	
cheeseboard; grated	

PORTUGAL

The climate of mainland Portugal may be unfit for cows, but sheep and goats happily exist on a diet of wild herbs and gorse blossom, producing thick, luscious milk to make the same exquisite cheese that has been produced for centuries.

With the exception of a few factories springing up in the 1960s to cope with tourist demand, Portuguese artisan cheese making has been virtually untouched. Small farms in remote valleys and mountainsides use ancient methods to ensure that each cheese retains its distinctive regional flavour.

One such method is the use of wild thistle leaves to coagulate the milk, a centuries old custom that gives Serra de Estrela cheese its unique taste and texture.

PORTUGAL

FACTS

Size
8cm diameter, 5cm high
Weight
200-300g
Fat in dry matter
45-55 per cent
When eaten
all year
In the shops
all year
Use
cheeseboard
Region
Setubal; Palmeal; Sesimbra

AZEITAO

A hand-crafted, award-winning cured cheese from the Arrabida valleys, Azeitao has been produced for several centuries and is much prized in Portugal. According to local history, the milk used to be stored in huge clay pots next to the fireplace, where it was left to curdle. Today, Azeitao is produced by cheese makers whose years of experience guarantee its typical characteristics. It is made with raw sheep's milk and, rather than using rennet, it is coagulated with a thistle flower. The rounds are covered in a pale orange rind, and the white or light yellow body has few or no holes. Its consistency is light and buttery, and it has a sweet, slightly piquant flavour. Serve it with wines such as Cabernet, Syrah, Pinot Noir or Rioja.

FACTS

Size
4cm diameter, 2cm high
Weight
100-200g
Fat in dry matter
50 per cent
When eaten
all year
In the shops
all year
Use
cheeseboard
Region
Alentejo

QUEIJO DE ÉVORA

Ewes reared in the town of Évora, in southern Portugal, produce the milk for this semi-hard cheese. The area has a distinctly Mediterranean agricultural climate with hot dry summers and lush pastures, which give the cheese its unique, rustic flavour. It is produced by coagulating the raw milk through the action of cardoon (*L. cynara carduncu-lus*) instead of rennet. The curds are then drained and bound. In 1989-90 this technique was investigated and perfected by the University of Évora.

Light yellow in colour, with few or no holes, the best Queijo de Évora has the scent and flavour of open pastures, oats and fresh hay, finishing with a slightly acidic tang. Production begins in November and peaks in March and April.

SÃO JORGE

São Jorge is a small volcanic island in the Azores, with high plateaux, craters, and lush pastures rich in wild flowers and herbs. Historically, settlers on the island produced cheese in order to maintain their independence when the Flemish colonized Portugal in the 15th Century. Islanders used traditional farmhouse methods of production and their cheese, which keeps well and improves with age, became popular with seafarers who stopped at the island. Transatlantic yachtsmen continue the tradition to this day. São Jorge looks similar to Gouda (page 148), but with the savoury tang of Cheddar and a hint of herbs and grasses. Made from unpasteurized cow's milk, it takes 120 days to mature, and has a hard, mottled yellow-brown rind.

FACTS

Size
15-20cm diameter,
8-10cm high
Weight
8-12kg
Fat in dry matter
45-50 per cene
When eaten
all year
In the shops
all year; sold in local
markets on São Jorge
Uses
cheeseboard; in sauces;
in salads and
sandwiches
Region
Azores

SERRA DE ESTRELA

Serra de Estrela has been in production since the 1100s, with an important role in the local economy of the Serra de Estrela region. The cheese is produced using fine ewe's milk from a single milking and it takes about three hours to make one cheese by hand: only two to three cheeses are produced in a single day. The cheese is solidified using thistle instead of rennet, which provides a fresh flavour that penetrates the pâte. The young cheese has a rich, buttery texture with a summery herbal taste, but once mature it becomes hard and sharp, whilst retaining a sweet, soft caramel undertone.

FACTS

Size
10cm diameter,
4-5cm high
Weight
900g
Fat in dry matter
45-55 per cent
When eaten
all year
In the shops
all year
Uses
cheeseboard; with milk
or coffee; mixed with
honey, pumpkin jelly,
pieces of walnut, hazel-
nut or almonds
Region
Beira

GREECE

In Ancient Greece, cheese was regarded as food for the gods and it was mentioned in Homer's *Odyssey*. But today, it struggles to retain its ancient status. Some sources claim that Greece consumes more cheese per head than France (it is a staple often eaten at all three meals).

Not surprisingly, quantity overtakes quality. Feta, Greece's most popular cheese, is bearing the brunt. Although good, rich Feta can still be found in a few areas of Greece and Turkey, mass-produced, salty factory Feta now fills the supermarket shelves.

However, lesser-known cheeses continue to be produced on a small scale.

In some remote regions, baskets for draining cheese are still hand woven as in ancient times; and in Crete and Naxos, a few traditional farms keep the art of cheese making alive. Among these artisan cheeses is the delicately flavoured Anthotiro, or 'flower cheese'.

GREECE

ANTHOTIRO

Anthotiro translates as 'flower cheese', so called because its delicate aroma and flavour carry a hint of the wild flowers and herbs grazed on by the sheep and goats whose unpasteurized milk is used to make it. A traditional farmhouse whey cheese, similar to Ricotta, it has been produced ever since the ancient Greeks developed inventive ways of converting whey into delicious cheeses. Milk is occasionally added to the whey to enrich the cheese. Anthotiro is manufactured in various shapes and sizes, particularly balls and truncated cones. It is smooth, hard and moist, with a fine, crumbly texture. The exterior is rindless, while the core is pure white with the characteristic flowery fragrance, overlaid by a smoky tinge. It is traditionally eaten for breakfast with honey, jam or fruit.

FETA

An account of how to make Feta is recorded in Homer's *Odyssey*, giving an indication of the cheese's historical roots. Traditionally made from sheep and or goat milk, Feta is soft, white and rindless. It can also be made from cow's milk, although that variety is often artificially whitened as the high fat content makes the cheese slightly yellow. Fresh milk is heated to around 35°C. Rennet is added and the mixture is left to coagulate. Once separated, the curd is broken and the whey drained off. The moist curds are pressed and salted, which makes the cheese firm. It is then left to dry before being packed in wooden barrels and covered in brine. Once in brine, Feta has a long shelf life and can be kept almost indefinitely. The finished product has a slightly acidic taste and salty flavour from the brine. It is used in cooking, as a table cheese and in salads.

GRAVIERA

The second most popular Greek cheese after Feta (page 122), Graviera can be made with cow's, goat's or sheep's milk, depending on the season. There are many different varieties, each with its own subtle, but generally rich, creamy, sweet and fruity flavours. Copied from Swiss Gruyère (page 142), it is hard with a supple texture and tiny holes. The rind bears a criss-cross pattern from the cloth in which it was drained. A connoisseur of Greek cheese should head for Crete where the Graviera, made from sheep's milk, is much sought after for its delicate fragrance and burnt caramel taste which becomes richer when the cheese is baked.
Alternatively, go to Naxos, where the milk has a delightful nutty flavour and is produced in a local co-operative.

FACTS

Size
20cm diameter, 15 cm high
Weight
2-8kg
Fat in dry matter
45-55 per cent
When eaten
all year
In the shops
all year
Use
cheeseboard; in pastries
Region
Dodoni; Naxos; Crete

KEFALOTIRI

Kefalotiri comes from the Greek word *kefalo*, which means hat, and indeed it has an unusual hat-like shape. It is also known as a 'first' or 'male' cheese, which indicates that it is made with full-cream milk, unlike the more delicate 'second' or 'female' whey cheeses. Kefalotiri dates back to Byzantine times and is made with sheep's milk, traditionally the first milk of the season after the lambs have been weaned. It is a hard, dry cheese with many irregular holes. The taste is fresh, with a distinct flavour of sheep's milk and a slightly piquant tang. Its pate and rind range from white to yellow in colour, depending on the mix of milk and the grazing. It has a ripening period of two to three months.

FACTS

Size
25-30cm diameter, 10-12cm high
Weight
6-8kg
Fat in dry matter
40-55 per cent
When eaten
all year
In the shops
all year
Uses
on pasta and salads; for grating; in *gratinée* dishes
Region
various

GERMANY

Germany has a gigantic cheese industry, but is far from being a cheese giant. Many of its cheeses are either processed cheese or copies of more famous European models, for example the popular 'German' cheese Limburger that in fact originated in Belgium.

However, the low plains of the North and the Alpine terrain of the South are ideal for producing high-quality milk, and the Bavarian cheeses, several of which share characteristics with their Swiss cousins, are excellent in their own right. Bavarian Bergkäse, for example, is a deliciously pungent cheese, and quintessentially German - it is eaten by the locals with beer and black bread.

BAVARIA BLU

This cheese is the result of German cheese makers spending centuries trying to tame the sharpness of the original German blue veined cheeses. It was introduced in 1972 as a 'new generation' blue cheese, with the unusual characteristic of having blue veins inside and a white mould on the outside – in German, Blauweissschimmelkäse.

How it's made
Penicillium roqueforti and *P. candidum* are integral to the process. The mould fungus and cheese mixture is allowed to mature for four to six days, then pierced with needles to introduce oxygen. The cheese is rubbed with mould spores in order to create internal blue veins, which become visible in eight to ten days. The cheese is then allowed to mature for a month or two at the unusually low temperature of 10ºC.

FACTS	
Size	Region
various	**Bayern**
Weight	
1.2 kg; 150g	
Fat in dry matter	
70 per cent	
When eaten	
all year	
In the shops	
all year	
Uses	
cheeseboard,	
salads, gratins	

Enjoying the cheese
This tangy, crumbly cheese is also surprisingly mellow. It is also deliciously creamy, as extra cream is added to the pasteurized milk. It is best on the cheeseboard with bread and fresh fruit, and paired with a robust, spicy red or demi-sec Sekt (sparkling wine).

ALLGÄUER BERGKÄSE (g.U.)

This typical Alpine cheese is made in Bavaria in traditional, creamery and farmhouse versions from unpasteurized
milk and only in the summer, when the cows are
grazing the mountain pastures, which is why it
is sometimes called Alpenkäse. Historically it
provided cowherds with a use for their surplus milk, and its affinage, starting on the
mountain and continuing in the valley,
takes four to 16 months. The rind is yel-
lowish-brown, growing darker with age,
and the interior supple to hard, ranging
in colour from ivory to light yellow
with an even distribution of occasional
holes. Bavarian Bergkäse is rich in
subtle flavours that suggest
fudge, hazelnuts and fruit, with
a creamy aftertaste.

LIMBURGER

Notorious as the smelliest of cheeses, Limburger is an adopted
rather than indigenous German cheese. It was created by
Trappist monks in Belgium, named after the town of Limburg,
then copied so effectively in 19th-Century Germany, that it has
been considered German ever since. The cow's milk curds are
sometimes washed in brine to reduce acidity, then lightly
pressed and moulded. The cheese is dry-salted or immersed in
brine, and turned frequently dur-
ing its maturation of six to
12 weeks. *Brevibacterium
linens* gives the rind its red-
dish-yellow colour. Inside it
is soft-textured, with
small irregular holes
and a strong, meaty
flavour, not as assertive
as the smell, but still an
acquired taste. Younger
cheese has a distinctive smell, but
doesn't stink. Serve with hearty rye
bread and onion.

GERMANY

DEUTSCHER EDELPILZKÄSE

This blue-veined semi-hard cheese is said to have originated at about the same time as the other famous blue cheeses of Europe. The name means 'cheese made with noble fungus' a reference to the *Penicillium roqueforti* used in its production. Edel-pilzkäse is predominantly mass produced, but one can find handmade versions that some connoisseurs consider world class. It is exported internationally under many brand names. The cheese is firm bodied compared to other German blue cheeses, for example Bavaria Blu (page 126).

How it's made
Pasteurized cow's, or sometimes ewe's, milk is used. The curd is heated, with care taken not to scald it. The whey is then drained and the curd is crumbled into large drums where it is dry salted. Stainless steel needles are inserted into the young cheese to allow air to penetrate. The cheese is then left to mature for five weeks in a foil wrap. When ready, it has a pale ivory pâte, striking dark blue veins and a coarse natural crust.

Enjoying the cheese
Edelpilzkäse is sweet, with a slight tang and perhaps a little gamey. It is particularly good in hot dishes and sauces, but will also hold its own on a cheeseboard. When young, it is soft and creamy, but as it ages it becomes firmer and crumbly. Eat it with sweet Auslese wine.

FACTS

Size	Region
various	**various**
Weight	
various	
Fat in dry matter	
55 per cent	
When eaten	
all year	
In the shops	
all year	
Uses	
cheeseboard, sauces	
and dressings	

MÜNSTER

Not to be confused with the cheese with a similar name: Munster (no umlaut) is made in France (page 69). Farm versions of Münster are made with unpasteurized cow's milk, whereas pasteurized milk is used for the creamery versions of the cheese. The reddish colour of the rind comes from bacteria. It has deep yellow flesh, a penetrating aroma and piquant taste. Smaller cheeses are only ripened for four to six weeks, and are milder. Farm Münsters are matured for a week outside before being transferred to caves with older cheeses. German Münster is eaten locally with potatoes and onions, or dark bread and beer.

FACTS

Size
**7-19cm diameter,
2.5-12cm high**
Weight
125-500g
Fat in dry matter
45 per cent
When eaten
**all year; farm version:
summer to winter**
In the shops
**all year; farm version:
summer to winter**
Uses
**cheeseboard; in sand-
wiches; quiche; raclette;
omelette; for
grilling**
Region
**Schwar-
zwald**

DEUTSCHER TILSITER

Dutch settlers in Tilsit, East Prussia (now part of Russia and Poland) accidentally invented this medium-hard cow's milk cheese in the mid-19th Century, whilst they were attempting to make their much-loved Gouda (page 148). The cheese became contaminated by yeast and moulds in the humid climate, and the settlers succeeded in creating a very different cheese with a thin, crusty dark-yellow rind, and a richer, more pronounced flavour. In farm and creamery wheels or loaves, the rind is washed and brushed repeatedly during the first two months of ageing, which keeps its smooth, elastic interior moist. Three months later, the cheese has developed a powerful aroma, and a creamy fruity taste, both of which intensify over time. Hearty bread and dark beers (if available) are excellent local accom-paniments.

FACTS

Size
**15-20cm long,
7cm high**
Weight
4.5kg
Fat in dry matter
30-50 per cent
When eaten
all year
In the shops
all year
Uses
**cheeseboard; in sand-
wiches; for grilling;
melted on potatoes and
other vegetables; in
sauces**
Region
various

GERMANY

QUARK

Hard to take seriously? This cheese not only shares its name with a subatomic particle, but a computer software; and in colloquial German, Quark means 'nonsense'. However: Quark was made in Germany before computers and atomic physics came on the scene and has long been extremely popular. Germans eat, on average, nearly 5kg a year each; it may account for almost half the country's cheese consumption. It's particularly versatile, being used in savoury and sweet dishes. 'Quark' literally means 'curds' – and that is what it is: the matter produced in the earliest stage of cheese making.

How it's made
Originally made by pouring soured cow's (or sometimes goats') milk into sacks and stowing them at room temperature overnight; in the morning the whey was squeezed out and the sacks were opened to reveal the Quark. Now, centrifugal force is used to separate curds and whey. Bacteria are added to the milk to start fermentation. Rennet is used to set it; this is a 'fresh' cheese - it takes only days to ripen.

Enjoying the cheese
If bought unwrapped, eat Quark as soon as possible after purchase; if pre-wrapped see the 'best before' date. It tastes fresh and creamy, with a slightly sour flavour. Try it with potatoes, on crusty bread or with red berries. Eat savoury Quark with beer, sweet with coffee.

FACTS	
Size	Region
various sized pots	**widespread**
Weight	
various weight pots	
Fat in dry matter	
0.5-40 per cent	
When eaten	
all year	
In the shops	
all year	
Uses	
on bread, dips,	
dressings, cooking	

ROMADUR

This is a close cousin of Limburger (page 127) and like its cousin, German cheese makers adopted it from Belgian Trappist monks in the 19th century. 'Romadur' probably comes from the Belgian *Remoudou*, or the Spanish *Ramdon*, both names of cheeses. It's smaller than Limburger, and milder: though aromatic, it lacks the pungent smell that puts some people off its cousin. It is sold in rectangular blocks, and is sometimes (like Limburger) known as the 'brick cheese'. Output is mainly industrial, but it is also made by hand, and this is one of the more interesting German cheeses.

How it's made
Similarly to Limburger. The curds, produced solely from Bavarian Alpine milk, are drained and then washed in brine. The bricks are at first stored together in order to encourage flora to develop on the rind. The ripening period of about two weeks is shorter than for Limburger. Afterwards, it must be kept cool to stop it getting over-ripe.

Enjoying the cheese
Romadur has a yellow-brown rind over a creamy golden pâte with small, irregular holes. It tastes sweet-and-sour, with a touch of smoke and less salty than Limburger. Some say it is best eaten with pumpernickel, sour cucumbers and beer - which foreigners find a quintessentially German experience.

FACTS	
Size	Region
Rectangular loaves of various sizes	**Allgäu (Bayern)**
Weight	
100-125g	
Fat in dry matter	
20-60 per cent	
When eaten	
all year	
In the shops	
all year	
Use	
cheeseboard	

GERMANY

WEISSLACKER

The Kramer brothers began making this cheese in the 1870s at their dairy in Oberallgäu, and today it is still only made at one dairy in the region. Weisslacker translates as white lacquer, probably a reference to the varnish of greasy mould on its surface, formed by the high salt content (8 per cent) leaching out. The pâte is very white, with a dense texture and occasional small holes. Similar to Limburger, it shares the same (to some) offensive smell.

How it's made

Skimmed evening milk is mixed with full cream morning milk. Once settled in the mould, it is placed in a brine bath for three days. Young cheeses are then stored touching each other to encourage bacterial growth on the surface. Ripening time is comparatively long: five months to a year, at high humidity, during which the cheese is regularly brine-washed.

FACTS

Size	Region
various	**Allgäu (Bayern)**
Weight	
Up to 1 kg	
Fat in dry matter	
40-50 per cent	
When eaten	
all year	
In the shops	
all year	
Uses	
eaten with beer,	
on bread	

Enjoying the cheese

The strong, salty flavour overpowers most wines, and this cheese (also called Bierkäse) is served with beer, especially Allgäu Hefeweizen (where available). Locals like it on rye bread with a slice of onion to complete the powerful flavours. If served on a cheeseboard, do so with compatible cheeses such as Romadur and Limburger. And store it away from other cheeses: it will contaminate its neighbours.

ALTENBURGER ZIEGENKÄSE (g.U.)

Ziegenkäse means goat's cheese, but the name is mildly ironic since the cheese is in fact a mix of cows' and goats' milk, which is rather unusual in Germany. Its origins can be traced back to the 19th Century, and the goats' milk content (15 per cent) is, by tradition, low: before refrigeration, goats' milk was hard to store. This is an East German cheese, but production stopped under the GDR's socialist government. Since 1990, it has been revived and granted g.U. (PDO) status and may be produced only at a handful of dairies in Altenburg and its surroundings.

How it's made
Caraway seeds are added before it sets, giving the distinctive flavour. After salting, the cheese is left to ripen for 10 days, and regularly treated with moulds to give a beautiful white bloomy exterior. It is extremely difficult to gauge the ripening process accurately, and all those attempting to copy the cheese have so far failed.

Enjoying the cheese
Its unassuming, spicy-sweet flavour has an after-thought of sourness. Essentially, it is a mild goat's cheese with complex overtones from the caraway seeds used in its manufacture. It is delicious when served on crusty bread and accompanied by a glass of German white wine.

FACTS

Size	Region
3-5cm diameter	**Altenburg and the**
Weight	**region; Sachsen,**
900g	**Thüringen**
Fat in dry matter	
30-45 per cent	
When eaten	
all year	
In the shops	
all year	
Use	
cheeseboard	

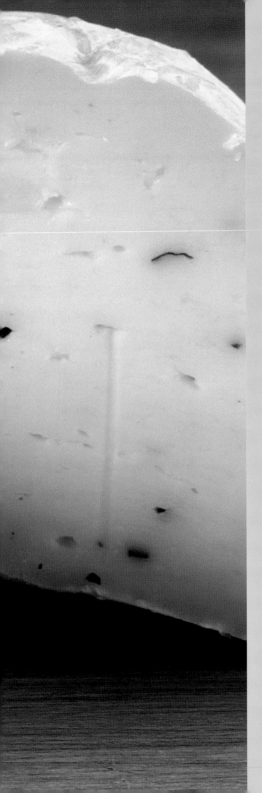

AUSTRIA

Only three cheeses are featured in this section, but this belies the lively tradition of artisan cheese making that survives in Austria. While this small country does not produce the internationally famous names, the amount of quality cheese produced is surprising.

There are a few basic cheese types, but many variations. For example, in the Bregenzerwald area of Vorarlberg alone there are more than 30 variations on the ubiquitous Bergkäse. This mountain cheese is influenced, like many in Austria, by those made in neighbouring Switzerland.

AUSTRIA

BERGKÄSE

Also made in Bavaria (see page 127), this smaller version originates in the Austrian Tyrol. The name simply means 'mountain cheese' and it is produced in a traditional Alpine wheel. It is made from unpasteurized milk in both farm-house and creamery versions, and only during the summer months when the cows (who are never fed silage) are at pasture. It is treated with brine twice a week, which produces a special rind mould that contributes to the sharp, aromatic flavour of the finished cheese. It matures in six months, after which the body is pliable to firm, depending on its age, with tiny holes. As well as being an excellent choice for the cheeseboard, it is a first-class melting cheese and, in some regional variations, is used in fondues.

KUGELKÄSE

From the Danube region, this is a simple, local, traditional and creamery cheese. Its name is appropriate: Kugel is the German word for ball, and the cheese is shaped into a small sphere. Made from cow's milk, the cheese forms a basic building block, its mild, unassertive taste ripe for the introduction of other flavours. Caraway seeds, pepper and paprika are added to the freshly formed curds, which are infused with the bouquet of the spices. The cheese is then hand-rolled into balls, which are salted and dried. They can be eaten fresh, but most are matured for two to three months. The spices give the Kugelkäse a speckled appearance, and their piquancy makes a delicious contrast with the delicate creamy flavour of the cheese.

MONDSEER

One of the oldest and most traditional cheeses in Austria, Mondseer has a washed rind and a pressed semi-hard pâte, and is also known as Schachtelkäse, because of the wooden box which is normally used to export it (*schachtel* being the German for box). Originally a monastery-made cheese, it is manufactured today in traditional and creamery versions, and is reminiscent of Münster (see page 129) and Limburger (page 127), but with a less pungent smell, firmer texture and milder flavour.

How it's made
The best cheese is traditionally made with whole or partly skimmed milk from cows whose diet is organic and silage-free. The curds are moulded and pressed, and the rind is dry-salted or brined, and treated with red-culture bacteria, *Brevibacterium linens*, before ripening for between four and 12 weeks in cool, damp cellars. The meticulous rind-washing is continued throughout the ageing period. Some cheeses are matured in foil or wax.

Enjoying the cheese
The finished cheese is covered with a dark orange peach-like rind, soft and downy with fine white mould. Its texture, though firm, is smoothly melting, and cooks well, without becoming rubbery or oily. As it ages, it becomes harder and crumblier, and its slightly piquant aroma and mild-sharp taste intensify.

FACTS	
Size	and melting; in
15cm diameter,	sauces
5cm high	Region
Weight	Salzburg
1kg	
Fat in dry matter	
45 per cent	
When eaten	
all year	
In the shops	
all year	
Use	
cheeseboard; in sand-	
wiches; for grilling	

SWITZERLAND

Like the Swiss army knife, Switzerland is more about quality than size. The majority of cheeses are still produced in mountain chalets or small farming co-operatives and must fulfil stringent criteria laid down by the Swiss Cheese Union.

Although cheese is no longer a currency in Switzerland (it was once used for trading with the Romans), it remains a crucial part of the Swiss economy, like tourism. Cattle are often fed indoors to ensure they don't eat trampled grass - and to keep the pastures looking good for the tourists.

To outsiders, perhaps Emmental is the typical 'Swiss cheese': a full-bodied cheeseboard cheese that also makes an incredibly rich fondue. (In the U.S.A., all cheeses with large holes are described as 'Swiss'.) But don't overlook others in these pages, for example Sbrinz, a hard cheese that beat Parmesan at a public tasting in 1998.

SWITZERLAND

APPENZELLER

A traditional Swiss cow's milk cheese, which is produced in wheels in Appenzell and the neighbouring cantons of St Gallen and Thurgau, Appenzeller is documented by tax records that go back more than 700 years. Inside a browny-orange rind, the smooth flesh has a pale, yellowish-orange colour and a firm texture, with a scattering of pea-sized holes. After making, it is bathed in a mixture of wine, spices and salt, which produces the hard, dry rind and gives it its distinctive spicy, fruity flavour that sharpens with age. Most cheeses are ripe in three to four months, but some are selected to be held for six to eight months and sold as Extra Appenzeller. The best cheese is made in mountain chalets from summer milk.

VACHERIN FRIBOURGEOIS

Fribourgeois is a traditional mountain cheese. It is one of the Vacherin family which includes several rich and creamy cow's milk cheeses from either France or Switzerland (see pages 82 and 145), and characteristically containing 45 to 50 percent milk fat. Fribourgeois, from the Swiss canton of Fribourg, has a greyish-yellow rind and a pale yellow, semi-soft interior. It is made from pasteurized milk that must come only from cows whose diet is free of any food additives: even silage is prohibited. After shaping, the cheese is brine-washed and then matured in very damp cellars for at least three months while the surface mould develops. Its firm body has a mildly acidic, savoury flavour, reminiscent of Gruyère, which increases when it's melted or grilled. Not to be confused with Vacherin Mont D'Or (page 145).

EMMENTAL

Although this quintessentially Swiss cheese, with its characteristic spread of gaping eyes, is now made elsewhere, its origins lie in the Emme Valley near Bern (*tal* is the German word for 'valley'). In a typical Swiss landscape of green hills, lush pastures and villages of wood chalets, the tradition of Emmental production has flourished for centuries in the skilled hands of alpine cowherds. Amongst the earliest documentary evidence is a mention that it was used in 1542 as compensation for the victims of a fire in Langehthal.

How it's made
Since such large quantities of milk are required to make Emmental, farmers work together as co-operatives. A mixture of unpasteurized evening and morning milk is heated in huge copper vats. The cheese is ripened in cool cellars, during which the famous holes are formed by trapped bubbles of gas produced by a special culture of bacteria. Affinage is usually four to 15 months (18 for a Réserve cheese).

Enjoying the cheese
Beneath a hard, dry golden-yellow rind the pâte is smooth, compact and creamy yellow. The mild aroma recalls freshly cut hay and the flavour, a combination of fruits and nuts, overlaid with an acidic tang. A glass of Sauvignon or Jura blanc makes the perfect complement.

FACTS

Size	Uses
80-100cm diameter, 16-27cm high	cheeseboard; in fondue
Weight	Region
75-100kg	central cantons
Fat in dry matter	
45 per cent	
When eaten	
all year	
In the shops	
all year	

GRUYÈRE (AOC)

The Swiss describe Gruyère as 'the cheese that never gets tired' because it has such a long shelf life and, as a result, exports well. As early as the 16th Century, it was being despatched to France and Italy, but its history dates even further back, to the 12th Century, when farmers would use it in lieu of rent due to the monks of Rougement Abbey. It melts beautifully, and is well known as the basic ingredient in fondue.

How it's made
As with Emmental (page 141), it requires large quantities of unpasteurized milk (400 litres for one 35 kg wheel), so farmers work together in co-operatives. The milk is from Fribourg cattle, and the cheese is moulded, pressed, brined and matured in cellars for between three and 12 months. At this stage, the cheese is turned regularly, and the rind brushed with brine to prevent cracking.

FACTS

Size	Uses
100cm diameter, 9.5-12cm high	**cheeseboard; in fondue**
Weight	Region
35-40kg	**Fribourg**
Fat in dry matter	
49 per cent	
When eaten	
all year	
In the shops	
all year	

Enjoying the cheese
The rind becomes tough, rusty brown and pitted with tiny holes. The cheese inside is straw-coloured, dense and grainy, also with small holes. Layers of complex flavours gradually assert themselves, beginning with fruity, and finishing with piquant. After a year's ripening, the taste is magnificently creamy and nutty, and the holes have shrunk further. Serve it with Merlot or Chianti.

SBRINZ (AOC)

For a cheese that has been around a long time, the origins of Sbrinz are the subject of, sometimes heated, debate. Some hold that it is what Pliny referred to as *caseus helveticus* in 100 AD; others that it was first recorded in trading records in Bern in 1530. Before any tunnels were dug, it was carried into Italy by sumpters, who returned with wine, spices and textiles. Made from whole cow's milk in the mountains of Central Switzerland in a similar process to Parmesan, the finished cheese has a brownish-yellow rind and a hard interior, with a compact, crumbly and granulated texture, white yellowish colour, and a salty, mellow and slightly spicy flavour. It is aged from two to three years (younger cheeses are called Spalen).

FORMAGGIO D'ALPE TICINESE (AOC)

Made since the 13th Century, this is the most significant cheese produced in the Italian-speaking Alpine canton of Ticino (Tessin in German and French) and the only one with AOC protection (gained in 2002). A typical mountain cheese, it traditionally provided herdsmen with a way of utilizing their excess milk until they descended from the high mountain pastures in the autumn. The cheese is still made in wheels every day between June and September, using time-honoured techniques, from raw cow's or goat's milk, or a mixture of the two, according to the tradition of specific valleys. The rind is very tough, ranging in colour from ivory to dark amber. Beneath it, the pâte is smooth and compact with a smattering of peanut-sized eyes and a deliciously fragrant, earthy flavour.

SWITZERLAND

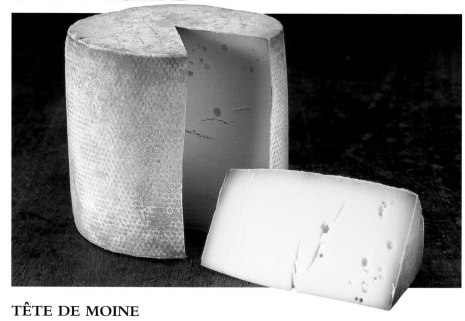

TÊTE DE MOINE

Originally called Bellelay, this Alpine cheese was devised by monks at Bellelay Abbey and renamed in the aftermath of the French Revolution. There is some debate over whether the phrase, Tête de Moine, meaning 'monk's head', refers to the tax levied against the farmers, who took over production from the monks, of one cheese per monk every season, or to the fact that, with its top cut off, the cheese resembles a monk's tonsure.

How it's made
Many small dairies throughout the Bernese Jura make Tête de Moine using time-honoured methods. Traditionally it was only produced during the summer (and sold between autumn and spring), but now it's made year round. They use rich unpasteurized cow's milk, mould the cheese into a cylinder and mature it for three to six months, during which the rind is repeatedly brine-washed.

Enjoying the cheese
The washings produce a sticky, terracotta coloured rind, beneath which the straw-yellow cheese is firm and silky with a pungent aroma. The intense flavour, at once fruity and meaty, is revealed when the cheese is served in the traditional way on a *girolle*, a wooden stand with a rotating blade, which pares off paper-thin slices into delicate rosettes. Accompany with Cabernet-merlot, a white Burgundy or stout.

FACTS	
Size	garnish on salads;
10-15cm diameter,	with pepper and
7-15cm high	powdered cumin
Weight	Region
700g-2kg	Berne
Fat in dry matter	
51 per cent	
When eaten	
all year	
In the shops	
all year	
Uses	
cheeseboard; as a	

VACHERIN MONT D'OR (AOC)

Although the French won the battle over who first made this luscious cheese (page 82), the Swiss officially retained the name, Vacherin Mont d'Or, from the Massif where it is produced. For generations, people recounted the myth of Roguin, a cowherd, who in 1871 drove a herd of cattle through the snow-bound Jura forests to aid General Bourbaki's retreating troops. He knew the secret recipe for Vacherin, settled in the pristine Joux Valley, and spread the word. Unfortunately recently uncovered documents record deliveries of Vacherins 26 years earlier in 1845.

How it's made
Made with pasteurized milk between mid-October and March, the cheese is cut into rounds and bound with a strip of red pine called a *sangle*. During its affinage on wooden planks in cellars, the cheese is turned and brine-washed daily. After four weeks, it is pressed into a pine box, which creates an attractive ripple across its golden crust.

Enjoying the cheese
The soft, raised, amber to reddish brown rind, covered with white fluff, protects a luxurious ivory-coloured cheese, with a creamy, delicate taste and hint of tannin from the *sanglage*. Eat it with a spoon straight from the box or add local white wine, cover with foil and melt in the oven to make a mini fondue.

FACTS	
Size	Uses
10-32cm diameter, 4-5cm high	cheeseboard; fondue
Weight	Region
500g-3kg	Vaud
Fat in dry matter	
50 per cent	
When eaten	
Aug to Mar	
In the shops	
AuG to Mar	

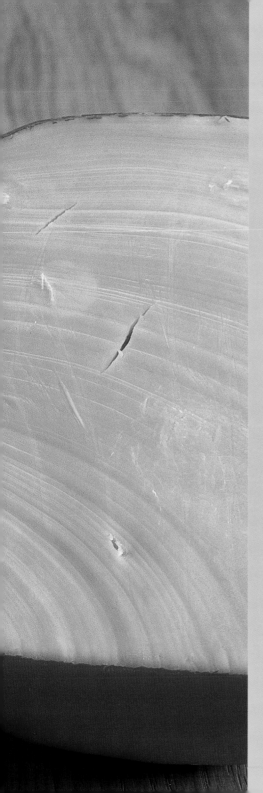

THE NETHERLANDS

Since the Middle Ages, when soldiers wore wooden Edam moulds as helmets in battle, Dutch cheese has been nothing if not versatile. In the 1840s, Edam is said to have been used as cannonballs in a Uruguayan ship. Whether or not you believe this, it is true that recently 10,000 spheres of the cheese were used to construct a model church in the town of Edam.

Cheese plays a major part in the Dutch economy: this small country is the biggest exporter of cheese in the world, meaning that artisan cheese makers are becoming increasingly marginalized. In the case of Leidsekaas, some may say this is a good thing - machines have now replaced the traditional method of treading spices into the curd with bare feet.

Of those artisan cheese makers remaining, most produce Gouda, staying faithful to a 6th-Century recipe that uses raw cow's milk and ages it for up to three years.

THE NETHERLANDS

EDAM

Edam is now manufactured throughout the Netherlands, but originated in a small town of the same name in Noord Holland, the one-time centre for Dutch cheese export. For most, its distinctive feature is the protective red coat, and formed either by dipping the cheese in, or spraying it with, wax. Generally, mild young cheeses without much character receive this treatment; exported Edams are red waxed, as in the illustration. Made from skimmed or semi-skimmed pasteurized cow's milk in a spherical shape, authentic Edam is normally six weeks old, with a firm but springy pâte, which is a sunny shade of yellow and has a subtly sweet, nutlike flavour. Cheeses aged for 17 weeks or longer are coated in black wax and have a more robust, concentrated taste. Authentic Edam, a rarer variety, has a natural rind but is much less widely available. After a year, Edam can become salty, but is still excellent for cooking.

AGED GOUDA

The best-known exported Dutch cheese was first made in the 6th Century on farms surrounding the small town of Gouda between Utrecht and Rotterdam, and was first manufactured for export 700 years later. It is made with whole cow's milk, pressed and brined. Aged Gouda can be differentiated from its younger sibling, by its black wax coating (the younger version usually has a yellow one), in marked contrast to the deep yellow interior, pitted with a few small holes. Aged Gouda may also be found with a natural rind. It is only considered 'aged' after a year's maturation, and 'extra aged' after 18 months, and can be matured for up to three years. When young, Gouda has a smooth, almost creamy texture and a gentle, nutty flavour, which grow grainier and more assertive in the mature cheese. Some Goudas are flavoured with cumin or herbs.

LEYDEN

This traditional farmhouse cheese from Leyden is made in a boulder shape with semi-skimmed cow's milk, mixed with a small amount (5 per cent) of buttermilk. Annatto is used to colour the curds, to which cumin or caraway seeds or cloves are also added. The curds are then pressed and dry-salted or brine-washed, and the rind is rubbed painstakingly with annatto until it shines. An authentic Leyden has an image of the crossed keys (the city's emblem) printed on its glossy orange rind. There is a delicious contrast of flavours between the powerfully aromatic spice and the nutty, buttery pâte.

Leyden is matured over several months in cool, moist cellars or curing rooms. It can also be aged for considerably longer than this and the best lasts for years. Enjoy it as the locals do, with dark bread and dark beer.

MAASDAM

A fruity nutty taste and irregular cherry-sized holes, both recalling Emmental (page 141), give Maasdam its nickname, the 'Dutch Swiss cheese'. A new creamery variety, it was created as recently as the early 1990s to provide an affordable alternative to Emmental, though it is moister and therefore plumper and more pliable. Made from cow's milk in a boulder shape, it has a semi-hard, deep golden-coloured pâte, and natural, smooth, polished rind (which is sometimes waxed).

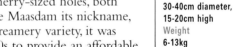

Maasdam matures more quickly than other comparable cheeses, needing only four to 12 weeks to be ready for consumption. Its sweet, unctuous flavour makes it a popular breakfast cheese in the Netherlands, where it's also a favourite for sandwiches. Leerdammer is one of the most famous brand-name producers of Maasdam.

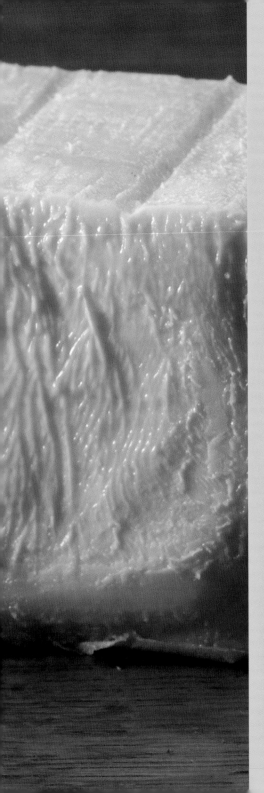

BELGIUM

Dwarfed by her cheese-giant neighbour, France, Belgium nonetheless has 250 different types of cheese, and though most are factory made, that is a serious number for such a small country. The industry had a surge in the 1960s, when it 'rediscovered' historic cheese recipes and tried to re-establish a national 'cheese identity'.

Traditionally made artisan cheeses are not impossible to find, however. Hervé is probably the best known Belgian cheese, available in the traditional unpasteurized form. Remedou is another highlight of this section, more piquant than Hervé, and often described by Belgians as 'stinking cheese'.

BELGIUM

HERVÉ

FACTS

Size
10cm long, 4cm high
Weight
200g
Fat in dry matter
45-55 per cent
When eaten
all year
In the shops
all year
Use
cheeseboard
Region
Liège

Made either with pasteurized or unpasteurized cow's milk, Hervé comes from the town of the same name and is probably Belgium's most famous cheese. Eat it quickly or be prepared to store it outside because its pungent aroma gathers strength as it ages. Makers sometimes add herbs to bring even greater piquancy to this effect. Shaped in small bricks, the russet skin owes its colour to the brining and the bacteria that gather on the outside during the three months' maturation in humid caves. Young cheeses are actually quite pale and sweet inside but, as the smell intensifies over time, the colour deepens and the taste becomes spicier. It is best eaten with a dark bread and with a dark beer to wash it down.

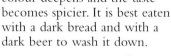

MAREDSOUS

FACTS

Size
various
Weight
800g-1kg
Fat in dry matter
45 per cent
When eaten
all year
In the shops
all year
Uses
cheeseboard; for grilling
Region
Namur and other regions

Made from cow's milk, the loaf-shaped Maredsous is a semi-hard pressed cheese. It gets its name from Maredsous Abbey in Belgium, where it is still made by the monks. It is while it matures in the monastery's cellars that the cheese acquires its characteristic colour, aroma, consistency and flavour. After the cheese has been lightly pressed, the cheese makers wash every one in brined spring water, removing the crust from the curds with a sponge. Later on the cheese is turned by hand while it develops its characteristic firm, orange crust and pungent aroma. Sometimes dusted with powdery white mould, the durable, well-formed rind protects the dense, supple, buttery texture of the interior, which releases flavours of grass and butter in a slightly sweet and sour combination.

REMEDOU

A cheese that takes no prisoners, Remedou is a Belgian, traditional, farmhouse and creamery, washed-rind variety made from cow's milk. The name of the cheese, also known as Remoudou, derives from *remoud*, the old Walloon word for the rich milk produced towards the end of a cow's lactation period. It is also known as 'stinking cheese' because of the surface bacteria that create the shiny, moist, rust-coloured rind and give the powerful aroma to this square-shaped cheese.

Remedou is a variation of Hervé, but larger and even more pungent as it takes longer to ripen. It's worth checking the weather forecast before embarking on a Remedou as it is best eaten in the open air with a glass of beer or really robust red wine to complement the strong flavour of the cheese itself.

FACTS

Size
various
Weight
200-675g
Fat in dry matter
40 per cent
When eaten
all year
In the shops
all year
Use
cheeseboard
Region
Liège

RUBENS

Rubens emerged from the 1960s revival of old Belgian cheeses, most of which were originally made in the monasteries before the Flemish farmers took over production. Today the 3 kg oval wheels are produced in traditional, farmhouse and creamery versions. Aptly named after the more famous Flemish painter, whose portrait decorates the label, this semi-hard washed-rind cow's milk cheese has an almost voluptuous taste, rich and smooth, and a supple, homogenous consistency. The pale yellow pâte has a generously filled look to it, with a scattering of small holes. It is encased in an even, reddish-brown rind, which has been washed and treated with red-culture bacteria. The cheese is ripened for approximately 45 days at a temperature of between 4 and 7°C.

FACTS

Size
30cm diameter, 9cm high
Weight
3kg
Fat in dry matter
50 per cent
When eaten
all year
In the shops
all year
Use
cheeseboard
Region
West Flanders

BRITAIN

'Many's the long night I've dreamed about cheese – toasted mostly', wrote Robert Louis Stevenson in Treasure Island, neatly (though unintentionally) summing up the dull image of the British cheese industry. This may be the fault of poor regulation of the 'cheddaring' process, resulting in a huge volume of mass-produced blocks of Cheddar, sadly giving British cheese a bad name. Yet a new generation of cheese makers is revitalizing the industry: James Montgomery's Manor Farm produces authentic Cheddar and Caerphilly, another victim of mass production, is now made again by artisan cheese makers. Today, England and Wales together can claim more than 500 traditionally made cheeses.

Scotland's harsh climate, rugged landscape and sometimes depressed economy saw its cheese industry almost at a standstill in the late 1800s, but in the 1980s it began to flourish again. Two highlights of this section are Cairnsmore, a deliciously moist cousin of Cheddar; and Bishop Kennedy whose rind is washed in – what else? – whisky.

HAND-MADE CHESHIRE

Mentioned in the Domesday Book of 1086, Cheshire is England's oldest named cheese, and was probably made by the Romans 1,000 years earlier. Today, since the 20th Century technological revolution, manufacture is almost entirely mechanized. One of the top producers of hand-made, calico-bound Cheshire cheeses is the Appleby family of Hawkstone Abbey Farm, and their cheese is pictured. With a history spanning several generations of cheese makers, they make their fine-quality classic Cheshire according to a traditional recipe with raw milk from their own farm, using open vats.

How it's made
The milled curd is placed in cylindrical calico-lined moulds and pressed. When removed from the mould, the cheeses are bound in calico cloth dipped in edible paste, which allows them to breathe and to ripen. Whilst they ripen for six weeks to six months, they are stored on shelves in the farm's maturing rooms at 13°C and 80 per cent humidity. During this period, they are turned and rubbed daily.

Enjoying the cheese
The farm's Friesian cows graze the salty summer pastures at the edge of the Cheshire Plain, which accounts for the cheese's rich, mellow, savoury flavour. The texture is firm, crumbly but never dry. It can be eaten young and mild or mature and stronger. Enjoy it with traditional English ale or a fruity Cabernet Sauvignon.

FACTS	
Size	Uses
20cm diameter, 30cm high	cheeseboard; melting; grilling; in sauces
Weight	Region
8kg	North Shropshire
Fat in dry matter	
48 per cent	
When eaten	
all year	
In the shops	
all year	

BEENLEIGH BLUE

One of only three blue sheep's milk cheeses made in Britain, Beenleigh Blue has won awards for its creator, Robin Congdon, who has been farming in the Sharpham area for the past 30 years. In an effort to find new outlets for his sheep's milk, he began by making yoghurt, and progressed naturally to cheese. He is a leading proponent of artisan cheese making, a tradition he helped to revive in the 1980s after it almost died out in the 1940s.

How it's made

From January to July, raw milk from Dorset-Friesland cross ewes is heat-treated before starter, rennet and a culture of *Penicillium roqueforti* are added. After resting, cutting, stirring and resting again, the curd is broken by hand and packed into moulds. After the surface has been salted, the cheese is spiked, allowed to blue, and wrapped in foil to discourage bad mould.

Affinage lasts for up to six or seven months.

Enjoying the cheese

Beneath a sticky rind, which reveals patches of blue, grey and white moulds, the body is the colour of ivory, shot through with bold blue-green veins. The texture is moist and crumbly, and the flavour penetrating and spicy, but not as salty as Roquefort. It discloses an underlying sweetness associated with ewe's milk. Cider is the perfect companion. (See also pages 163, 166 and 178.)

FACTS	
Size	Uses
20cm diameter,	cheeseboard; salads;
15cm high	sauces
Weight	Region
2.7kg	Devon
Fat in dry matter	
52 per cent	
When eaten	
Aug to Jan	
In the shops	
Aug to Jan	

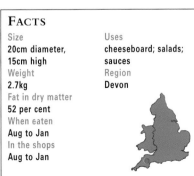

BRITAIN: ENGLAND AND WALES

BERKSWELL

Dairy and sheep farmer Stephen Fletcher became a cheese maker in 1990 through a quirk of fate, when a local shop, having lost its goat's cheese supplier, asked him if he could make ewe's milk cheese. He rose to the challenge, inventing his own cheese based on a traditional recipe for Caerphilly. Hand-made at the Fletchers' 16th Century farmhouse, Ram Hall, at the edge of Berkswell village, the eponymous cheese quickly established its own distinctive character, and has received numerous awards.

How it's made

The raw milk of the Fletchers' Frieslands is heated in small vats. Vegetarian rennet is added, after which the curd is cut, scalded and stirred, removed from the vat, and placed in a basket mould. The cheese is repeatedly turned, salted and brushed with a protective coating, which aids moisture retention and reduces cracking. The cheese matures on shelves in a temperature-controlled store, where it is turned regularly, for three to eight months.

Enjoying the cheese

The natural rind is tough and rusty-red, and bears the impression of its basket mould. When aged, it roughens with ridges and pits. The pâte is hard, granular and chewy. The flavour, which is as round and complex as that of a mature Pecorino (pages 97–99) or Manchego (page 111), suggests roasted nuts, sweet onions and wild flowers.

FACTS	
Size	Uses
20cm diameter, 8cm high	**cheeseboard; grating; in soups**
Weight	Region
3-4kg	**West Midlands**
Fat in dry matter	
45 per cent	
When eaten	
all year	
In the shops	
all year	

FARMHOUSE CAERPHILLY

Affectionately referred to as one of 'the crumblies', this (usually) raw cow's milk cheese originated in a Glamorgan village in about 1830. A small salty, moist wheel, designed to be eaten young, it was the traditional lunch of Welsh miners, effectively replacing the salt and moisture they lost in sweat. Although small-scale farm production was common in South Wales in the 19th and early 20th centuries (and has lately been revived), Welsh Caerphilly became mass-produced after World War II. Old-fashioned farmhouse production was revived first in south-west England.

How it's made
Starter is added to the warmed milk, which is left to ripen before the temperature is gradually raised. It is renneted, cut, stirred and scalded. The particles then break cleanly. The curd is allowed to settle before draining, is swept into piles, 'textured' by cutting into increasingly smaller pieces, salted, and placed in linen cloths in moulds. It is lightly pressed, drained and rested, followed by brining and ripening in a damp cellar over one to two months.

Enjoying the cheese
Beneath a leathery ivory-white rind, dusted with grey-white moulds, the pâte has a firm, pliant texture and fresh, citrus tang when young, but grows crumblier and the flavour more rounded with age. It is excellent with dark bread and traditional ale.

FACTS	
Size	Uses
18cm diameter, 6cm high	**cheeseboard; melting; Soufflé; Welsh Rarebit**
Weight	Region
400g-4kg	**Ceredigion; Dyfed; Somerset**
Fat in dry matter	
48 per cent	
When eaten	
all year	
In the shops	
all year	

CELTIC PROMISE

Winner of a clutch of awards, including British Cheese Supreme Champion in 1998, this smear-ripened cheese is made by John Savage-Onstwedder of Teifi Farmhouse Cheese (see page 86). He produces it using a recipe created with the late trail-blazing cheese maker, *affineur* and guru, James Aldridge, founder of the Eastside Cheese Company. Celtic Promise is a semi-soft cheese, made with unpasteurized cow's milk, and shaped like a dumpling.

How it's made
The starter is home-made and the rennet vegetarian, and, when the curd has set, it is cut, washed and scalded twice. After draining, it is put into moulds and pressed. It is removed from the moulds and smeared - as opposed to washed - with brine and then cider. The cider smearing is repeated as it ripens over about eight weeks, to promote the growth of the orange-pink moulds essential to its character.

Enjoying the cheese
The cider imparts a pungent, fruity aroma to the cheese and gives it its smooth, orange-pink rind, with a powdery coating of white mould. The deep yellow interior has a compact, soft texture and rich, sweet-sour and spicy flavour. Enjoy it on the cheeseboard, ideally with a jug of farmhouse cider.

FACTS	
Size	**Region**
12cm diameter, 7cm high	**Ceredigion, Wales**
Weight	
500-650g	
Fat in dry matter	
48 per cent	
When eaten	
all year	
In the shops	
all year	
Use	
cheeseboard	

CERNEY

Artisan cheese maker Lady Angus used to make a range of specialist, award-winning unpasteurized goat's milk cheeses, named after her Cotswold village, and still owns the business. Her cheese-making pedigree is impeccable, having learnt the craft from a farmer's wife in Valençay, where the cheese (see page 83) was her inspiration for Cerney. The creamery is in a converted farmhouse close to Lady Angus's Chapel Farm.

How it is made
Full-cream milk is bought in, and the cheese made daily. The mould is in the shape of a truncated pyramid. The cheese is sprinkled with a special oak ash and sea salt mixture, imported from Valençay, which forms a speckled outer layer. It is allowed to rest and, as the cheese absorbs the salt, it releases moisture. It matures in the fridge for between five days and two weeks or longer.

Enjoying the cheese
If eaten young, the cheese is fresh, mild and lemony, with only a faint hint of goat. As it matures, it remains smooth and creamy, but develops a more emphatic, goaty and rounded flavour. An ageing of one to two weeks is considered ideal. Other versions of Cerney include the self-explanatory Smoked, Pepper and Ginger, Banon (brandy-washed and wrapped in vine leaves) and Starter (intended for cooking).

FACTS	
Size	Region
7cm square base, 4cm square top, 7cm high	Gloucestershire
Weight	
240g	
Fat in dry matter	
43 per cent	
When eaten	
all year	
In the shops	
all year	
Use	
cheeseboard	

DAYLESFORD ORGANIC CHEDDAR

An enterprise of Sir Anthony and Lady Bamford, (of the JCB family) Daylesford Organic is more than a mere cheese maker, it is an organic estate, with a farm, kitchen gardens, restaurant, café, bakery, farm shop and creamery. The milk from its herd of Friesian cows is taken directly from the milking parlour to the creamery, where the prize-winning Cheddar is hand-made by Joe Schneider in rounds and truckles, using traditional methods of production. The rind is rubbed to encourage the bloom, and the cheese is wrapped in cloth and aged for a minimum of nine months. The mature cheese has its own discrete personality: muscular with a sharp bite at the start, followed by a slow, deep, mellow finish. Despite its traditional English heritage, this Cheddar is now a specialist cheese and produced in small quantities.

DELICATUS

A fine, hand-crafted, raw goat's milk cheese from John Jenkin's Mar Goats on St Michael's Farm, Delicatus embodies his ethos that: 'A happy, well-fed animal which has been well cared for produces excellent milk and the result is a first-class cheese.' The goats are milked twice a day in the farm's purpose-built milking parlour. The flavour of the goats' rich diet of sweet hay, fruit, flowers, herbs and hedgerows is perhaps more evident in Delicatus than in any other of the Mar Goat cheeses. There are also overtones of beech wood, from the shelves where the cheese is left to mature. The texture is firm, and as it ages, the rind is washed with brine, ensuring a pronounced tangy flavour.

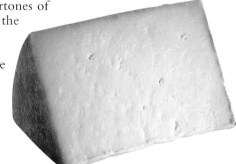

DEVON BLUE

Robin Congdon invented his only cow's milk cheese in the mid 1980s, and has been making Devon Blue ever since. The pasteurized milk comes from the farm's own herd of Ayrshires, and the production process is similar to that used for Beenleigh Blue (page 157). The mould added is *Penicillium roqueforti*, and the curd is cut twice, first coarsely and then finely, with a wire device called a 'harp'. It is not drained but placed directly in the moulds. The cheese is salted, spiked and, after several weeks, wrapped in foil. After an affinage of four to eight months, it is moist, buttery and crumbly with a more reticent flavour than Ticklemore's other blue cheeses, recalling leather, herbs, grass and cream, overlaid with the piquant tang of the blue. (See also pages 166 and 178.)

FACTS

Size
**20cm diameter,
15cm high**
Weight
3kg
Fat in dry matter
53 per cent
When eaten
all year
In the shops
all year
Use
cheeseboard
Region
Devon

FINN

Finn is one of two cow's milk cheeses made by Neal's Yard Creamery, and its only matured cheese, hence the name, which means 'white ancient one' in Irish Gaelic. It is made with unpasteurized, full-fat cow's milk, which Charlie Westhead, who runs the creamery, collects himself from the September Organic Dairy at nearby Almeley. It is one of the few triple cream cheese produced in England. Ten per cent of cream is added to the milk, with the starter and penicillin mould for the rind, and the cheese is matured for two to four weeks, after which it is dense, creamy and remarkably rich. The rind is coated in a billowy white mould, and the flavour is gentle, clean and faintly acidic, with a suggestion of mushrooms.

FACTS

Size
**Approx 7cm diameter,
3cm high**
Weight
200-225g
Fat in dry matter
60 per cent
When eaten
all year
In the shops
all year
Use
cheeseboard
Region
Herefordshire

DORSET BLUE VINNY

Production of this traditional Dorset skimmed-milk cheese almost ceased in the 1970s, until Michael Davies of the Dorset Blue Cheese Company single-handedly revived it. Vinny - or Vinney as it was usually spelled - comes from the obsolete word 'vinew', which meant mouldy. As skimmed milk cheeses have too little fat to encourage the moulds, they are difficult to blue, and, in the days before controlled spores could be added to milk, cheeses would harden and spoil.

How it's made
Raw milk from Woodbridge Farm's Friesian herd is skimmed by hand to reduce its fat content. *Penicillium roqueforti* mould and vegetarian rennet are added. After the curds have been cut, milled, salted and packed into moulds, they are left in the warm dairy to encourage blueing. The cheese is turned, unmoulded, covered with flour and blue-mould paste and matured for ten weeks to five months. If necessary, after one month, it is spiked.

FACTS	
Size	grilled; in soups and
Approx 20 cm	sauces
diameter, 30 cm high	Region
Weight	**Dorset**
6 kg	
Fat in dry matter	
40-46 per cent	
When eaten	
all year	
In the shops	
all year	
Uses	
cheeseboard; melted;	

Enjoying the cheese
Its low fat content accounts for its light, crumbly texture. The fine blue veins extend from the outside throughout the pâte, which darkens with age. The dominant flavour is mellow and nutty, with a penetrating sharpness concentrated in the pockets of blue and a lingering aftertaste. Pair it with a glass of tawny port.

DOUBLE GLOUCESTER

Records show that this unpasteurized cow's milk cheese had its origins in the 8th Century, and has been made in Gloucestershire and elsewhere since the 16th. Its name may refer to its size - bigger than Single Gloucester (page 175) - or the fact that it's made with the full-cream milk from both morning and evening milkings. Traditionally produced as a large wheel, it has a thick natural rind, which had to withstand local cheese rolling ceremonies. Cheese merchants used to test its strength by jumping on it: if it didn't crack, it was safe to travel.

How it's made
The vegetable dye, annatto, is added to the milk with the starter. This gives the cheese its orange colour, originally produced with carrot juice or saffron. In farm-made versions, after draining, the cheese maker traditionally tests the consistency by biting the cheese to see if it 'squeaks'. If so, it's ready for milling. Affinage takes two to six months.

Enjoying the cheese
The cloth used to wrap the cheese as it ripens leaves its imprint on the tough rind, which is coated with grey-blue moulds. Underneath, it is firm, smooth and pungent, similar to Cheddar, but with a more robust, buttery flavour from the double rich milk, overlaid with an orangey tang. It is delicious with a Rioja or a Riesling.

FACTS	
Size	Uses
varies greatly between makers	**cheeseboard; grating; grilling; in sauces**
Weight	Region
3.5-8kg	**Gloucestershire; Shropshire**
Fat in dry matter	
48 per cent	
When eaten	
all year	
In the shops	
all year	

BRITAIN: ENGLAND AND WALES

FLOWER MARIE

FACTS

Size
6cm square, 5cm high
Weight
200g
Fat in dry matter
50 per cent
When eaten
all year
In the shops
all year
Use
cheeseboard
Region
East Sussex

The makers of Golden Cross (see page 167), Alison and Kevin Blunt of Greenacres Farm, also produce this square-shaped, soft white, ewe's milk cheese. They buy in the unpasteurized milk from a farm in Dorset. The late great cheese lover and expert James Aldridge conceived the recipe for Flower Marie, aptly named because of its perfumed creaminess, in collaboration with the Blunts, using the Corsican cheese Fleur de Maquis as a model (see page 51). The cheese is brined before it is left to mature for two to six weeks, during which time it is turned. The rind is bloomy white tinged with pink, and the flesh, which melts in the mouth, has an intense flavour that blends aromatic herbs, flowers, grass, caramel and citrus with a hint of mushroom.

HARBOURNE BLUE

FACTS

Size
20cm diameter, 15cm high
Weight
3kg
Fat in dry matter
48 per cent
When eaten
all year
In the shops
all year (can be unavailable winter to early spring)
Use
cheeseboard
Region
Devon

Twice medal winner for Robin Congdon and his partner Sari Cooper at the British Cheese Awards, this pioneering goat's milk cheese is Ticklemore's most recent addition to their range and already one of their most popular. Pasteurized full-fat goat's milk is used, and it's made in truckles, in almost exactly the same way as Beenleigh Blue and Devon Blue (see pages 157 and 163). It needs three to four months to mature, after which the sweet-smelling interior is white, threaded with blue veins, and it has the emphatic, spicy taste typical of blue cheeses. As Robin himself admits, Harbourne Blue can vary considerably in strength throughout a season. Since it can overwhelm milder cheeses, it is advisable to serve it alone afterwards, accompanied by a robust wine.

GOLDEN CROSS

Sainte-Maure de Touraine (page 77) provided the inspiration for this award-winning soft white, raw goat's milk log, made by Kevin and Alison Blunt of Greenacres Farm (also page 166). They devised the recipe with a French neighbour, Regis Dussatre, who sold them his milking parlour. The Blunts are devoted to their goats, a mixture of British Saanens and Toggenburgs, who kid twice a year, guaranteeing almost continuous milk supply and cheese production.

How it's made
Like Sainte-Maure, coagulation takes 24 hours and the curds are gently ladled into a long mould to form a log. Unlike Sainte-Maure, vegetarian rennet is used, no straw is necessary (as Golden Cross is a firmer-textured cheese), and it is rolled in charcoal rather than ash. The charcoal encourages the penicillin moulds to develop, and after several days a furry coating forms on the rind. It matures for two to eight weeks.

Enjoying the cheese
Aficionados consider Golden Cross at its best after a six-week maturation, when its texture, beneath a velvety white rind, is as smooth and soft as ice-cream and just beginning to run at the edges. The taste balances the sweetness of caramel and vanilla with the acidity of grass. Try drinking with Sancerre.

FACTS	
Size	Uses
3-4cm diameter at one end, 4-5cm diameter at other end, 14-16cm long	cheeseboard; grilled in salad
Weight	Region
225-250g	East Sussex
Fat in dry matter	
45 per cent	
When eaten	
all year	
In the shops	
all year (limited in autumn and winter)	

KEEN'S CHEDDAR

Brothers George and Stephen Keen are third-generation farmers and cheese makers at Moorhayes Farm, which their grandfather took on in 1900. Cheddar cheese originated almost 500 years earlier in the 15th Century, when it was matured in the Cheddar Gorge caves. Over the centuries British - especially Somerset - cheese makers have become very experienced in Cheddar production, developing and refining it; no other country has produced it so successfully. Keen's traditional Cheddar stands out for its particularly rich, full-bodied texture and succulent, savoury taste.

How it's made
They use full-fat unpasteurized milk from their home-bred cattle, and animal rennet. The cheese is pressed three times, for 24 hours each time. Between the first two pressings, it's dipped in hot water, to encourage the rind. After the second pressing, it's rubbed with lard, and wrapped in two layers of muslin, then left to mature for ten months to two years.

FACTS

Size	grilling; grating; souf-
40cm diameter,	flé; quiche; sauces
30cm high	Region
Weight	Somerset
25 kg	
Fat in dry matter	
48 per cent	
When eaten	
all year	
In the shops	
all year	
Uses	
cheeseboard; melting;	

Enjoying the cheese
After ideally a year, Keen's Cheddar has a perfect moist, pale yellow interior, and a creamy, nutty flavour with a sting on the finish. Opinions differ on what to drink with it: many choose a serious Bordeaux; others only contemplate Guinness.

LINCOLNSHIRE POACHER

Simon Jones has broken out of the mould with this 1996 Supreme Champion, as it's the only cheese to be produced in Lincolnshire, a county unconducive to dairy farming. Simon is the fourth generation to run his family farm, on chalky land at the edge of the Wolds, where the grazing is surprisingly fertile. As the summers tend to be dry, the cheese is made from October to July. In 1992, the late famous Welsh cheese maker Dougal Campbell helped to create the recipe, based on his own Tyn Gryg cheese.

How it's made
Full-fat unpasteurized milk from the farm's own herd of Holstein cattle is used. Warm morning milk is mixed with cold milk from the previous evening. After the curd has been cast into moulds, it is pressed for 48 hours. Truckles are turned out and matured on wooden boards for 12 to 24 months, during which they are turned regularly to ensure even maturation throughout each cheese.

Enjoying the cheese
Beneath a natural rind that looks like granite, the interior is firm, resembling Cheddar. When young, it has a gentle, sweet-bordering-on-fruity flavour with earthy overtones, whilst more mature cheese is rich with a bitter-sweet tang and lingering aftertaste. Pair it with Rioja or Sauvignon Blanc.

FACTS	
Size	grilling; grating;
Truckle: 30cm	**sauces**
diameter, 30cm high	Region
Weight	**Lincolnshire**
Truckle: 20kg	
Fat in dry matter	
45 per cent	
When eaten	
all year	
In the shops	
all year	
Uses	
cheeseboard; melting;	

LLANGLOFFAN

Leon Downey was co-principal viola player with the Hallé Orchestra until 1977, when he made the life-changing decision to retire and become a cheese maker in rural Wales. With his traditional cow's milk Llangloffan, he has been instrumental in reviving Welsh farmhouse cheese making. Named after the hamlet where it is hand-made, it has twice won the British Cheese Award for Best Welsh Cheese. A natural performer, Leon stages cheese-making demonstrations, where he keeps large audiences spellbound.

How it's made

There isn't space on the Downeys' farm to keep enough cows, so they buy in full-fat unpasteurized milk locally. Leon uses an original, liquid starter and vegetarian rennet. He also makes a flavoured version of Llangloffan, adding chives and garlic with the salt during milling, and the natural red dye, annatto. The cheese is placed in cloth-lined moulds, pressed and matured for at least ten weeks, and up to ten months.

Enjoying the cheese

The stone-coloured rind shows the imprint of the cloth in which it is moulded, and the interior has a firm yet rather dry, almost crumbly texture that dissolves on the tongue. The flavour, depending on its age, is gentle and grassy with a spicy aftertaste.

FACTS	
Size	Uses
Small: 25cm diameter, 10cm high; large: 75cm diameter, 30cm high	cheeseboard; melting; grilling; grating; sauces
Weight	Region
Small: 4.5 kg; large: 13.5 kg	Pembrokeshire
Fat in dry matter	
53 per cent	
When eaten	
Oct to May	
In the shops	
Oct to May	

MONTGOMERY'S CHEDDAR

The Montgomery family has been making cheese at Manor Farm for almost 100 years and three generations: James is the dedicated present incumbent. He produces ten to 15 truckles of classic Cheddar a day, made from the raw milk of his Friesian herd. The loamy Somerset soil provides wonderfully fertile pasture, and the cheese has an incomparable flavour, recognized by the high number of its British Cheese Awards.

How it's made
A starter is added to the chilled evening and warm morning milk. The process known as 'Cheddaring' is accomplished by hand. It involves gathering the drained curds into blocks and repeatedly stacking them to expel the whey, and gives the finished cheese its tight texture. After salting and milling, it is pressed, larded, wrapped in cheesecloth and matured on a wooden shelf for six to 24 months, during which it is turned regularly.

Enjoying the cheese
The cheesecloth encourages a gradual loss of moisture and produces its firm, creamy, slightly flaky texture. The rind moulds influence the cheese from the outside in, slowly releasing flavour. It is beautifully balanced: mellow waves of nut, fruit and grass are followed by a strong, but not bitter, lingering tanginess. Drink it with a fine Cabernet Merlot or Zinfandel.

FACTS	
Size	Uses
40cm diameter, 30cm high	**cheeseboard; melting; grilling; grating; soufflé; quiche; sauces**
Weight	Region
26kg	**Somerset**
Fat in dry matter	
48 per cent	
When eaten	
all year	
In the shops	
all year	

MRS KIRKHAM'S LANCASHIRE

Mrs Kirkham's mother and grandmother also made Lancashire, a cheese whose history stretches back several hundred years when meat was expensive and it became a staple of the poor. Ruth Kirkham follows traditional methods that produce a depth of flavour and texture sorely missing from mass-produced versions. For real Lancashire cheese, as made by Mrs Kirkham, the process is unique among English cheeses.

How it's made
Unpasteurized, cooled evening milk is added to warm morning milk; a starter culture and then rennet is added; the curd is cut by hand and allowed to settle to keep as much fat as possible. The whey is drained off and the curd transferred to another container where it is broken several times. The next morning, curd from each of the three previous days is mixed in equal quantities. The curds are milled, salted, moulded, pressed, bandaged between pressings, buttered and matured for four to eight months.

FACTS	
Size	Uses
30cm diameter,	cheeseboard; toasting;
30cm high	in apple tart or pie
Weight	Region
12kg	Lancashire
Fat in dry matter	
48 per cent	
When eaten	
all year	
In the shops	
all year	

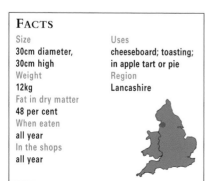

Enjoying the cheese
Mrs Kirkham's is considered by many to be the finest Lancashire available. It has a thin, golden rind and moist, creamy texture, which hardens and becomes crumblier with age. The pâte is pale with a pleasing piquancy. It has a silky texture when melted. Pair it with Chianti, Sauternes or Tawny Port.

RAGSTONE

Another award-winning raw goat's milk cheese made by Neal's Yard Creamery, Ragstone differs from Perroche by being matured. It is moulded into a log shape by being placed upright in a tall pipe, so it is effectively pressed by its own weight. It ripens over a two to three week period, although it may be kept for a further two weeks. The finished cheese has a billowy white mould rind and a creamy, dense yet slightly crumbly texture, and is reminiscent of Sainte-Maure de Touraine (page 77). After a short affinage, the flavour is light, fresh and lemony, but never sharp. The longer it ripens, the richer the texture and more forceful, goaty and saline the taste become. It grills beautifully.

SHARPHAM

It is the quality of the milk from Debbie Mumford's organically farmed Jersey cows that gives this cheese its smooth, rich texture and distinctive, robust flavour. The herd grazes lush pastures bordering the river Dart, and Debbie uses their fabulously creamy milk, fresh and unpasteurized. The cheese is hand-made in Sharpham Creamery's new purpose-built dairy to a 1980 recipe. The only additions are starter, vegetarian rennet and salt. The curds are ladled into the moulds by hand, and after draining, the cheese is brined and turned. It matures for seven to ten weeks, after which a velvety white mould has formed over the rind, and it has the faint aroma of mushrooms and a surprisingly powerful but fresh taste of grass and herbs.

SHROPSHIRE BLUE

One of the younger English cheeses, Shropshire Blue was created in the 1970s by Scotsman and trained Stilton-maker Andy Williamson. In its original incarnation, made in Scotland, it was called 'Inverness-shire Blue' or 'Blue Stuart', but was sold throughout the rest of Britain as Shropshire Blue. This was a misnomer, as it had no connection with the county. Now made by Stilton makers around the country, it is a firm, creamy cheese with green-blue veining, reminiscent of Stilton, with an orange-coloured pâte.

How it's made
Hand-made from full-fat pasteurized cow's milk with vegetarian rennet, following a recipe and production process similar to Stilton's (see page 176), it differs in having the vegetable dye annatto added to the milk, with the starter and *Penicillium roqueforti*. The annatto is responsible for the deep orange-brown rind and for the colour of the pâte. It is matured for at least 12 weeks, or longer to produce a creamier, fuller-bodied cheese.

Enjoying the cheese
It has a smooth, semi-hard, quite loose texture, a strong aroma and rich, mellow flavour with an underlying tanginess. It is crumblier and sharper tasting than Stilton, but has a finish full of caramel sweetness. Partner it with a robust red wine, Port or traditional English ale.

FACTS	
Size	sauces
20cm diameter,	Region
30cm high	Derbyshire;
Weight	Leicestershire;
8kg	Nottinghamshire
Fat in dry matter	
48 per cent	
When eaten	
all year	
In the shops	
all year	
Uses	
cheeseboard; soups;	

SINGLE GLOUCESTER

Gloucester cheese production is concentrated around the Vales of Gloucester and Berkeley, where possible using milk from Gloucester cows, which are now exceedingly rare. Of the two types of cheese, Double Gloucester (page 175) is the better known, because it keeps longer and therefore travels better. Smaller, crumblier and milder flavoured, the Single is more economical to make, traditionally with the evening's skimmed milk combined with a small amount of whole milk from the following morning. It has a natural rind, and is produced in a flat disk shape.

How it's made
Traditional cheese makers generally choose unpasteurized milk and a vegetarian rennet. Methods are similar to those used for Double Gloucester, although the curds are cut into smaller pieces, producing a more acidic cheese. After scalding, they are drained, milled, salted, moulded and pressed for several days. Usually matured for two months.

Enjoying the cheese
Small variations in the way different producers make the cheese result in distinctive flavours. Generally, the texture is light and the flavour gentle. Wick Court's has a clean taste and silky texture; Smart's is fresh, chewy and tangy; whilst Charles Martell's is luscious and creamy.

FACTS	
Size	grated
20cm diameter,	Region
7cm high	**Gloucestershire**
Weight	
truckle: 2-4kg	
Fat in dry matter	
48 per cent	
When eaten	
all year	
In the shops	
all year	
Uses	
cheeseboard; melted;	

STILTON

England's 'king of cheeses' has been made exclusively in three Midlands counties since the 18th Century, but never in Stilton. The name arose because the landlord of Stilton's Bell Inn, a staging post between London and Scotland, served his customers with a succulent blue cheese made in his family. The flavour and texture of Stilton are so highly regarded that it is one of the British cheeses with a certification trademark.

How it's made
Stilton is made from pasteurized local cow's milk, to which rennet and *Penicillium roque-forti* are added. Moulds are cylindrical, and turned daily for five or six days, ensuring an even distribution of moisture and the flaky, open texture essential for blueing. The cheese is unmoulded, smoothed by hand, and ripens for nine to 15 weeks. The turning continues, and at about six weeks it is pierced with stainless steel needles, allowing air to enter and circulate within the cheese.

Enjoying the cheese
Beneath the crust, the cheese is smooth and buttery with a network of distinctive green-blue veins. The flavour is mellow, spicy and full of lingering complexity. Traditional at Christmas, Stilton is excellent with port, Sauternes or a robust red wine.

FACTS	
Size	sauces; dips; salad dressing; in salads
20cm diameter, 30cm high; 'baby': 15cm diameter, 20cm high	
	Region
Weight	Leicestershire; Nottinghamshire; Derbyshire
7-8kg; 'baby': 2.5kg	
Fat in dry matter	
48 per cent	
When eaten	
all year	
In the shops	
all year	
Uses	
cheeseboard; soups;	

STINKING BISHOP

At Laurel Farm in the 1970s, Charles Martell almost single-handedly revived the Gloucester breed of cattle, which was nearing extinction. He started making cheese as a way to publicise its plight, but now has to buy in Friesian milk from a local farm to supplement his supply. Stinking Bishop is based on a washed-rind cheese made long ago by Cistercian monks on Charles's own land. Although the name is apposite - the smell is often compared to old socks - it actually derives from the variety of pear used to make the perry, the liquor with which the rind is washed.

How it's made
The milk is usually pasteurized. The curds are drained but not milled, and ladled into moulds. To increase the moisture content and encourage bacteria, salt is added after the cheese has been removed from the mould. While it matures for six to eight weeks, it is washed repeatedly in perry.

Enjoying the cheese
Similar to Epoisses (page 60), it has a sticky yellow-orange rind and a soft to runny, creamy pâte, which becomes harder and crumblier at certain times of the year. The flavour, though robust, is not as strong as the pungent aroma suggests. Drink it with Burgundy.

FACTS	
Size	Region
20cm diameter, 4cm high	**Gloucestershire**
Weight	
2kg	
Fat in dry matter	
48 per cent	
When eaten	
all year	
In the shops	
all year	
Use	
cheeseboard	

TICKLEMORE

Robin Congdon has always enjoyed a challenge in his cheese making, and particularly likes to tackle unusual varieties. Ticklemore, his own invention, is a hard goat's milk cheese, one of only a handful produced in Britain. It is moist and firm textured, though crumbly at the centre, with a sweet, subtle flavour and no pungent aroma of goat. Made from pasteurized whole milk, it is pressed flat by hand into a colander, which gives it its distinctive flattened sphere shape. It is dry-salted and matured for approximately ten weeks. The natural dimpled rind, with marks from the colander, forms as it ripens. As waves of grass, herbs and soil hit the taste buds, it reveals a character seldom found in goat's cheese. (See also pages 157, 163 and 166.)

TORNEGUS

Legendary cheese maker and founder of the Eastside Cheese Company, James Aldridge, who died in 2001, had his greatest success with this smear-ripened cheese. He put its invention down to an accident. While he was maturing an unpasteurized Duckett's Caerphilly near some Stiltons, some orange bacteria from the Stilton rind passed into the Caerphilly. A customer who tasted it thought the result delicious. The name combines 'tor' (suggesting the Caerphilly's Somerset origins) and 'negus', a spiced fortified wine. James's partner, Pat Robinson, has been making it since his death. She marinates the Caerphilly in lemon verbena and mint, brine and local wine, and matures it for ten weeks, during which she massages the rind to spread the bacteria.

TYMSBORO'

Dr Mary Holbrook gave up archaeology to become a farmer and cheese maker in the Mendips. The unpasteurized milk for her cheese comes from the 90 goats she home-rears, a perfect mix of British Saanen, British Alpine and Anglo-Nubian. The untreated pasture on Mary's Sleight Farm is rich in nettles, thistles and other vegetation, which produces high-quality milk. She only milks the goats between spring and autumn when they are grazing. The cheese has the same truncated pyramid shape as Valençay (page 83), as well as a light coating of salted charcoal powder, overlaid by greenish penicillin moulds, which develop over its three to four week affinage.

FACTS

Size
7cm square base, 4cm square top, 7cm high
Weight
200g
Fat in dry matter
45 per cent
When eaten
late spring to winter
In the shops
late spring to late autumn
Use
cheeseboard
Region
Somerset

WESTCOMBE CHEDDAR

One of the newest of the traditional style, hand-made, cloth-bound Cheddars, Westcombe is produced by farmer-turned-cheesemaker Richard Calver. Although he only established Westcombe Dairy as a producer of traditional cylindrical cheeses in the late 1990s, there is evidence of cheese making at the farm going back to the 1890s. He uses raw milk from his own Friesian-Holstein cattle, which enjoy lush grazing within a mile of the dairy. Richard produces about 100 rounds a week, ageing each for up to 20 months. Pale in colour, and tinged with gold, the finished cheese has a wonderful soft, close-knit texture. The flavour is delicate, yet complex, and fruity but with a strong, peppery kick from the ageing and a lingering aftertaste.

FACTS

Size
40cm diameter, 30cm high
Weight
24-25kg
Fat in dry matter
48 per cent
When eaten
all year
In the shops
all year
Uses
cheeseboard; melting; grilling; grating; soufflé; quiche; sauces
Region
Somerset

WATERLOO

Most cheese makers come to the craft through farming, but Anne Wigmore has a scientific background. She runs her business, Village Maid, with husband Andy, and is responsible for creating four new varieties of cheese: Spenwood (a hard sheep's milk), Wellington (a hard Guernsey, now discontinued), Wigmore (see page 182) and Waterloo. With all her cheeses, she was eager to create entirely new recipes, rather than use existing ones. As a result her cheeses are all unique. Gold medal winner in the 2003 British Cheese Awards, Waterloo is creamy soft, made with unpasteurized milk from Guernsey cows, which the Wigmores buy in from local farms.

How it's made

Rather than drained, the curds are washed and ladled into moulds so that the whey and water flows out. They are not pressed, but stacked in piles, turned, remoulded and stacked again. The cheese is rubbed lightly with dry salt and brine. Its affinage takes between four and ten weeks: four to six being the optimum time for perfect creaminess.

Enjoying the cheese

The natural rind, with its light coating of mould greys and wrinkles with age. The rich Guernsey milk gives the cheese its luscious, golden interior, which tastes sweet and fruity, with hints of earthiness, but turns peppery as it matures.

FACTS	
Size	Use
15cm diameter, 5cm high	**cheeseboard**
Weight	Region
900g	**Berkshire**
Fat in dry matter	
45 per cent	
When eaten	
all year (although scarce)	
In the shops	
all year (although scarce)	

WENSLEYDALE

The history of this crumbly cheese with a sweet lingering flavour dates to the arrival in England of French Cistercian monks who followed William the Conqueror in the 11th Century, and settled in Wensleydale. The damp Dales' caves were ideal for ripening their blue cheese, made with ewe's milk. During the 14th Century cow's milk was introduced as a substitute, although a little ewe's milk would be added to retain the open texture and ease blueing. Nowadays, white Wensleydale is much more common than the blue.

How it's made

Most current farm producers use cow's milk, although some prefer sheep's. For the latter, the curds have to be cut coarsely as sheep's milk tends to dry out if it is cut too finely. It is usually ripened for four to eight weeks, or three to six months for the mature variety. Smoked and flavoured versions are also produced.

Enjoying the cheese

White Wensleydale is usually eaten young, when it is fine-textured, flaky and moist (mature Wensleydale is drier). Yorkshire's limestone soil gives the cheese a gentle flavour, beautifully balanced by an underlying and slightly tart freshness. It is traditionally eaten with fruitcake or apple pie, and complemented by a medium-dry white wine.

FACTS	
Size	tarts; bannock; cake
15cm diameter,	Region
15-20cm high	**Yorkshire**
Weight	
5kg	
Fat in dry matter	
45 per cent	
When eaten	
all year	
In the shops	
all year	
Uses	
cheeseboard; soups;	

WIGMORE

Anne and Andy Wigmore's eponymous cheese is made from ewe's milk, a variety that was popular before the Dissolution of the Monasteries. The Wigmores - and their Village Maid Cheese company - have played an important role in the reintroduction of sheep's milk cheese to Britain (it had almost disappeared by the 18th Century), and their reputation for originality is demonstrated in their decision to make this semi-soft cheese - traditionally these cheeses were hard. Wigmore's fine texture and subtle balanced flavour have earned it three gold medals at the British Cheese Awards.

How it's made

The Wigmores buy in unpasteurized ewe's milk from farms in Warwickshire and Northamptonshire, and use vegetarian rennet. They wash the curds, as they do for Waterloo (see page 180), and pack them into the moulds to drain, a process that produces a less acidic cheese. The cheese is ripened for between two and three months.

Enjoying the cheese

The pale brownish, bloomy rind has a rumpled appearance, yeasty smell and soft, yet slightly chewy consistency. It hides a luxurious, elastic pâte, peppered with eyes, which starts to flow in a more mature cheese, and slowly reveals an array of delicate, memorable flavours, including caramel, nuts, milk, flowers, grass and herbs.

FACTS	
Size	Use
15cm diameter, 4-5cm	cheeseboard
cm high; 'baby': 10cm	Region
diameter, 4cm high	Berkshire
Weight	
1.4-1.8kg; 'baby': 450g	
Fat in dry matter	
48 per cent	
When eaten	
all year (but scarce)	
In the shops	
all year (but scarce)	

YORKSHIRE BLUE

Judy Bell of Shepherd's Purse is best known for her sheep's milk cheeses, which she started making in 1989 to provide an alternative for people with allergies to cow's milk. She revived the ancient tradition of making sheep's milk Wensleydale in her Original Farmhouse version (see page 181). Made to her own recipe for an equally traditional blue Wensleydale, Yorkshire Blue shows her diversifying into cow's milk cheese (she finds sheep's milk increasingly hard to obtain). Judy had to devise her own recipe because the cheese had been extinct for so long, that none existed.

How it's made
Judy uses pasteurized milk from local farms and vegetarian rennet. As the monks who introduced Wensleydale to England in the Middle Ages used Roquefort as their basis, so does she, adding *Penicillium roqueforti* to the milk with the starter. The moulds she uses are pieces of drainpipe, which shape the cheese into a perfect tall cylinder. It is pierced and, after a month, wrapped in foil. Affinage lasts about three months.

Enjoying the cheese
If eaten young, it has the mild, sweet, creamy flavour and crumbly texture typical of Wensleydale, although there is a subtle tang concentrated in the blue veining. Mature versions are buttery, with a more emphatic flavour.

FACTS	
Size	Region
20cm diameter, 10cm high	**Yorkshire**
Weight	
3.5kg	
Fat in dry matter	
48 per cent	
When eaten	
all year	
In the shops	
all year	
Use	
cheeseboard	

BISHOP KENNEDY

Based on the 'trappist' cheeses created by medieval monks in the monasteries of France, this modern, creamery, washed-rind cheese in the shape of a disk takes its name from a 15th Century bishop of St Andrews. It is made by Howgate Cheese in Kinfauns with full-fat pasteurized cow's milk and vegetarian rennet. To give the cheese an appropriately Scottish character, the rind is washed liberally with malt whisky during its eight-week maturation. Repeated washings encourage the rind to develop into a distinctive sticky, orangey-red crust. The cheese inside has the texture of velvet, which starts to run as it ripens. Its aroma is emphatic and musty ('old socks' is a common verdict), and it brims with flavour that is both powerful and creamy, with a satisfyingly spicy finish.

CAROLA

Passionate organic farmers and cheese makers, Nick and Pam Rodway produce various cheeses for their company, Wester Lawrenceston Cheeses, using unpasteurized milk from their small herd of Ayrshire cattle. The company is named after their 24-hectare mixed farm perched above the Moray Firth. In the dairy, Pam is an intuitive self-taught cheese maker, and she and Nick formulated their recipe for the award-winning Carola, with traditional croft-made cheeses in mind. They also borrowed the production process, but this time from across the Channel in the form of Tomme (see page 81), as it's moist and full of flavour. Beneath a thin, supple rind, Carola has a delicate, creamy yellow interior with a crumbly semi-soft texture and sweet, subtle flavours of heather, gorse and herbs that gradually unfold.

CAIRNSMORE

Galloway Farmhouse Cheese's excellent modern, hard cheese is hand-made with unpasteurized milk from its own flock of Friesland ewes, and named after a local mountain. Only made between April and October, the cheese is ripened for six months - unusually in vacuum packs, which slow down its maturation - after which some cheeses are waxed, some flavoured, some smoked and others selected for longer affinage. (The flavoured and smoked versions are waxed later.) After a further four months, the rind of the matured version has hardened and become encrusted with striking red moulds. The pâte is softer, creamier and more moist than most hard sheep's milk cheese.
The bouquet suggests old leather
and the flavour is sweet,
fragrant and
nutty with
the caramel
overtones
typical of
sheep's milk.

FACTS
Size
18-20cm diameter, 4 or 10cm high
Weight
100g portions; 1-2kg
Fat in dry matter
55 per cent
When eaten
all year
In the shops
all year
Use
cheeseboard
Region
Wigtownshire

GLEN MORAY

This is Nick and Pam Rodway's washed-rind version of their original Carola cheese (see opposite). It was commissioned by Glenmorangie in celebration of the local single malt whisky, which it owns. Both cheeses are made in exactly the same way, in flattish rounds from the raw milk of the Rodway's own organic Ayrshires. The sole difference is the repeated rind-washing with the eponymous single malt during Glen Moray's maturation. The rind-washing promotes the growth of *Brevibacterium linens*, which
give this cheese its characteristic
pink-tinged rind and, as the
moulds penetrate the rind,
mellowing the interior, a
sweeter, richer and
creamier flavour. The
cheese is kept humid, so
that it doesn't dry out.
Don't be put off by its
challenging aroma: the taste
is less emphatic than the
smell.

FACTS
Size
various
Weight
800g-1kg
Fat in dry matter
45-55 per cent
When eaten
all year
In the shops
all year
Use
cheeseboard
Region
Moray

LANARK BLUE

Humphrey Errington's flock of several hundred Friesland sheep graze the lush hillsides above the upper Clyde valley. He uses their milk, unpasteurized, to make this Roquefort-style artisan cheese, which he created in 1985 and is recognized as one of Scotland's finest modern varieties. Threaded with blue-green veins, it has a powerful salty taste and a creamy white interior, and is one of three cheeses, all handmade in Humphrey's farmhouse creamery.

How it's made

Vegetarian rennet and *Penicillium roqueforti* culture are added to the milk. After moulding, the cheese is dipped in brine twice. It is matured for twelve weeks in a cool, humid atmosphere, and turned three times a week so that it never has to be pressed. After four or so weeks, it is wrapped in foil to inhibit further rind mould. The cheese is scraped before it is wrapped for sale.

Enjoying the cheese

The taste of the cheese differs markedly from one season to the next, as clover and herbs replace grass in the sheep's pastures. Cheese made in the spring and summer has a creamy, medium-full flavour, whilst the winter variety is more forceful and robust. The milder cheese pairs well with a sweet white Bordeaux, and the stronger goes perfectly with a full-bodied Shiraz.

FACTS	
Size	on oatcakes or with
various	apples
Weight	Region
1.4-1.8kg	Strathclyde
Fat in dry matter	
45 per cent	
When eaten	
all year	
In the shops	
all year	
Uses	
cheeseboard; crumbled in salads; in dressings and sauces;	

LOCH ARTHUR

Hard cheeses, requiring a long maturation, have always dominated Scots cheese making, where the short season meant that the cheese had to be able to survive the severe winter. Well-suited to the environment, this traditional farmhouse Cheddar is made by Barry Graham and a team from the Loch Arthur Creamery, part of the Camphill Village Trust, a community for adults with special needs near Dumfries. Among a fistful of medals, it won gold at the 2001 British Cheese Awards.

How it's made
The Creamery uses fresh unpasteurized milk from their own herd of organic, bio-dynamically reared Ayrshires, to which vegetarian rennet is added. Rather than sticking the cheesecloth to the cheese with lard or flour paste, Barry employs the traditional method of 'scalding', which makes de-clothing difficult, but produces a deliciously nutty flavour. Produced in cylinders, Loch Arthur is matured for six to 12 months.

Enjoying the cheese
A pale brown-grey natural rind surrounds a firm, fairly dry cheese, best eaten young. The flavour is not so emphatic as most traditional English Cheddar, but is wonderfully multi-layered: floral, nutty and spicy on the finish. The Creamery produces a drier, but more aggressively flavoured miniature cheese at Christmas time, as well as a smoked version throughout the year.

FACTS	
Size	Region
various	**Dumfries and**
Weight	**Galloway**
9kg	
Fat in dry matter	
48 per cent	
When eaten	
all year	
In the shops	
all year	
Uses	
cheeseboard; for grating, grilling and melting; in sauces	

IRELAND

You would expect one of the wettest, and in parts, lushest, countries in Europe (national colour, green), to have had a continuous history of cheese making - especially as it is a major producer of milk and butter.

In fact, serious cheese making has only re-surfaced in recent decades.

In Northern Ireland most cheese is factory produced, not made on a farm, leaving the Republic, particularly west Cork, in the far south-west, to lead the way in artisan, specialist cheese making.

Among the highlights of this section, either as fresh inventions or adapted from old recipes, are Milleens, Gubbeen and Ardrahan (all three produced in County Cork); and the Gorgonzola-like Cashel Blue, famed for its voluptuous taste.

ARDRAHAN

Known for its unique flavour, this modern washed-rind cheese is made by Mary Burns at her family-run farm in Duhallow. The family started making farmhouse cheeses by accident in the 1970s, when Mary's late husband, Eugene, realized that in order to find healthy food for his family, he had to make it himself. The milk comes from the farm's herd of pedigree Friesians, founded in 1925 by Eugene's father from the best in the UK. The lush grazing that surrounds the farm is reflected in the name, which means 'height of the ferns'.

How it's made
Mary keeps the precise recipe a secret. But we know that the curds are cut by hand, moulded, in lengths of pierced piping for the smaller cheeses, and repeatedly turned. When set, the cheese is brined in a bath of salt water and matured for four to eight weeks.

Enjoying the cheese
Encrusted with colourful rind moulds, the cheese has the pungent, earthy aroma typical of washed-rind cheese. The interior is golden and buttery with a deliciously deep, lingering flavour that becomes definitely nutty the more it ages. Because hand-made, each cheese has its individual taste, and varies slightly in size. It is traditionally eaten in cubes with a glass of Irish whiskey.

FACTS	
Size	other vegetables; in
19cm diameter,	cooking
3.5-4cm high	Region
Weight	County Cork
1kg and 300g	
Fat in dry matter	
49 per cent	
When eaten	
all year	
In the shops	
all year	
Uses	
cheeseboard; melted	
over potatoes or	

CASHEL BLUE

Ireland's first farmhouse blue cheese takes its name from the Rock of Cashel, which surveys the Tipperary plains near Louis and Jane Grubb's dairy farm. They invented the cheese in the 1980s, while investigating ways to use the surplus milk from their pedigree Friesians. Cashel Blue is now in such demand that they have to buy in extra milk. Much of the cheese is sold young, when it's firm and crumbly, but for a softer texture and more complex flavour, it needs to be matured for three months.

How it's made
The milk is usually pasteurized and inoculated with *Penicillium roqueforti*. After cutting and draining, the curds are moulded and turned until they are dry enough to be salted and pierced. The cheese is rotated on a turntable and pierced with long needles, which promotes development of the blue mould. The mould is washed off the outside before the cheese is wrapped in gold foil.

Enjoying the cheese
The finest cheese is made when the cows are out to pasture between April and October, and has an inimitable, aromatic flavour with a pleasant tang but no salty sharpness. Though firm and moist when young, the aged version (up to six months) is mouthwateringly creamy with a deep, mellow flavour. Pair it with a Sauternes.

FACTS	
Size	Region
20cm diameter, 12cm high	**Tipperary**
Weight	
1.5kg	
Fat in dry matter	
54 per cent	
When eaten	
all year	
In the shops	
all year	
Uses	
cheeseboard; melted; in sauces and salads	

IRELAND

COOLEA

FACTS

Size
**25-30cm diameter,
10cm high**
Weight
4kg and 10kg
Fat in dry matter
45 per cent
When eaten
all year
In the shops
all year
Uses
cheeseboard; in sauces
Region
County Cork

Originally from the Netherlands, the Willems brought a cheese recipe with them when they settled in County Cork. Helen's original plan was to start painting straight away but it was 15 years before Dick, her son, could finish his training in Belgium and give her enough time off from making this Gouda-style full-fat cow's milk cheese. Traditional rennet and pasteurized milk from Friesians are used and an added coating both prevents mould developing and aids ripening. Never younger than six months, young Coolea has a distinctly sweet taste of wild meadow. The older cheese is the more complex adding a tang of peat as it reaches its maximum maturity at two years, enough to hold its own on the cheeseboard even with blue cheeses.

CLONMORE

FACTS

Size
**25cm diameter,
7.5cm high**
Weight
2.5kg
Fat in dry matter
45 per cent
When eaten
autumn and winter
In the shops
autumn and winter
Use
cheeseboard
Region
County Cork

Tom Biggane started making this semi-hard, mature Gouda-style cheese with the help of a Dutch friend in 2000, and it took him two and a half years to adapt and perfect. Made in large wheels with milk from Tom's own small herd of goats, it is now hugely popular, particularly in Ireland, and was a gold medal winner at the Listowel Cheese Awards in 2003. The goats graze outside, so the cheese is only produced during the summer, and the milk is pasteurized. The ideal maturing time is between four and five months, after which it has acquired a subtle goaty aroma and a remarkable depth of flavour with strong hints of nuts and fruit.

DURRUS

A raw milk washed-rind cheese, Durrus is produced in County Cork by Jeffa Gill who originally intended to farm organically and sell a range of produce. From modest beginnings with a pan on the stove in her own kitchen, she now takes her milk from the Friesians of two local families as demand for this delicious semi-soft cheese overtook the output of her own cows. Made in a copper (rather than stainless steel) vat, Durrus is mild and creamy with a coral pink rind when young, and takes on more strength and character as it matures, acquiring a fruitier flavour. It is ready to be sold in three to five weeks but will keep for up to five months, by which time it will be flowing.

FACTS

Size
large: 18cm diameter, 6cm high; small:10cm diameter, 5cm high
Weight
large: 1.5kg; small: 380g
Fat in dry matter
57 per cent
When eaten
all year
In the shops
all year
Use
cheeseboard
Region
County Cork

GABRIEL

Bill Hogan makes cheese for his West Cork Natural Cheese company on the beautiful, lush Mizen Peninsula at Ireland's southern-most tip. Bill was a student of the late Swiss cheese maker Josef Dubach in Costa Rica, and adheres strictly to Dubach's principle of making cheese exclusively during the four summer months, when the grass is at its lushest and the cow's milk of superior quality. Bill buys in raw milk from seven local farms. The unique dairy is painted a vibrant turquoise, which, he says, deters flies. Gabriel, one of three cheeses they produce is made in sharp-edged wheels. Matured for one to two years, it is firm and grainy, not unlike Parmesan (page 98), with a well-developed fruity flavour and peppery aftertaste.

FACTS

Size
35cm diameter, 10cm high
Weight
6kg; giant: 25-45kg
Fat in dry matter
48 per cent
When eaten
all year
In the shops
all year
Uses
cheeseboard; on pasta; in sauces or fondue
Region
County Cork

IRELAND

FACTS

Size
20cm diameter, 5cm high
Weight
1.5kg
Fat in dry matter
48 per cent
When eaten
all year
In the shops
all year
Use
cheeseboard
Region
County Cork

GUBBEEN

The name comes from the Gaelic word 'gobin', which means small mouthful and refers to the bay, west of Schull, where the Fergusons' farm stands. Tom's family has farmed here for five generations, and Giana has been making cheese for 20 years. Due to the Gulf Stream, West Cork benefits from a warm, damp climate, perfect conditions for pasture. Their herd – a mix of Friesian, Simmenthal, Jersey, Shorthorn and Kerry cattle – is kept outside grazing for eight months of the year. Giana makes cheese every day, using traditional methods. She dilutes the whey to decelerate bacterial activity, and is painstaking over turning and brining the cheese during its maturation. Beneath a wrinkled grey-peach rind, it has a smooth, supple texture and is clean-tasting with savoury overtones.

FACTS

Size
22cm diameter, 3-4cm high; 'dotes': 10cm diameter, 3-4cm high
Weight
1.5kg; 'dotes': 200g
Fat in dry matter
45 per cent
When eaten
all year
In the shops
all year
Use
cheeseboard
Region
County Cork

MILLEENS

Depressed by the lack of interesting food within striking distance of the mountainous Beara Peninsula, Veronica Steele started making this artisan, Trappist-style washed-rind cheese in 1976 and single-handedly forged a tradition of modern Irish farmhouse cheese making. With her husband Norman, she makes Milleens from the whole milk of Friesian cows, and never forgets the important scientific basis at the heart of her craft. The complex, subtle flavour of the cheese is at once piquant and aromatic from the heather and grasses of the peninsula's mountains and pastures where the cattle graze. It has a mottled rind, which ranges from pale pinkish to vibrant orange, and the pâte inside can be creamy or runny, but doesn't flow like some soft cheeses. It is matured for four to ten weeks.

MINE-GABHAR

Ann and Luc van Kampen produce this unpasteurized, vegetarian cheese from the 100 or so goats kept on their farm in a remote corner of County Wexford with more milk bought in from two other farms. Soft and smooth, but not liquid, it has a sweet, positive taste but not of goat: flowers and woodland in the spring come first to mind. Vegetarian rennet and home-made starter are used sparingly to produce the small, round cheeses which are then sprayed with penicillin to induce the velvety white coating which starts to grey with age. The van Kampens' other cheese, Croghan, is mild and semi-soft with hints of herbs and sea-salt. Neither cheese is made between November and May as kidding is not artificially scheduled for winter milk.

FACTS	
Size	**6-8cm diameter, 2-3cm high**
Weight	**225g**
Fat in dry matter	**45-55 per cent**
When eaten	**Jun to Oct**
In the shops	**Jun to Oct**
Uses	**cheeseboard; grilled; in salads**
Region	**County Wexford**

ST KILLIAN

At 17 Paddy Berridge was taught how to make Camembert in the kitchen of the handsome house where he was brought up on Carrigbyrne Farm in County Wexford. Ten years later he went into the business professionally, producing a hexagonal-shaped full-flavoured Camembert made with pasteurized cow's milk from the farm's own herd of Friesians and, now, using vegetable rennet. Joined almost at the outset by Alan Girot, his cheese maker, they have developed a medal-winning cheese that is mild when young, growing in character and natural flavours as it ages.

The penicillin-induced bloom is not affected by the brining at the end of the manufacturing process because they use iodine-free salt. St Killian goes extremely well with red wines such as Beaujolais, Burgundy, or claret.

FACTS	
Size	**10-12cm diameter, 2-3cm high**
Weight	**250g**
Fat in dry matter	**45 per cent**
When eaten	**all year**
In the shops	**all year**
Use	**cheeseboard**
Region	**County Wexford**

DENMARK

This flat country, rich in green meadows, seems designed to make cows happy, and in fact these factors give Danish cheese its identity: the output is almost entirely semi-soft cows' milk cheeses.

Denmark's economy relies heavily on food exports, and has developed many cheeses according to demand: the 1960s, for example, saw the creation of several nondescript creamy cheeses, some adapted from neighbouring countries, to give markets what they wanted.

Danish Blue is the most popular outside Denmark, with its distinctive salty tang and creamy texture. However, Danes consider Samsø their classic cheese. It originated in Switzerland, but is the basis for many other Danish cheeses and the cheese of choice for the Danish open sandwich.

DENMARK

FACTS

Size
20cm diameter, 10cm high
Weight
3kg
Fat in dry matter
50-60 per cent
When eaten
all year
In the shops
all year
Uses
cheeseboard; in salads; in dressings
Region
various

DANISH BLUE

Also called Danablu and Marmora, Danish Blue was invented in the early 20th Century by Marius Boel, and became a tremendously successful alternative to Roquefort: it is now sold all over the world. A creamery semi-soft cow's milk cheese, in a drum or block shape, it is milder and less complex than its older competitor. Its pale white interior is shot through with fine blue-green veins, which overlay its creamy flavour with a sharp, salty taste. The cheese takes 60 to 90 days to ripen and, like all blue cheeses, becomes more pungent with age. The rind is white to yellowish and slightly moist. A very versatile cheese, which cuts easily and can be crumbled or spread, it's excellent with fruit (especially pears and peaches), salads, dark breads and red wines.

FACTS

Size
15-20cm long, 6cm square
Weight
2-4.5kg
Fat in dry matter
45-50 per cent
When eaten
all year
In the shops
all year
Uses
cheeseboard; in sandwiches; for grilling and melting; Danish fondue
Region
various

HAVARTI

This semi-soft Danish cheese was created in the 19th Century by cheese maker Hanne Nielsen, who studied methods employed in other European countries and then came home to put some fizz into the rather dreary cheese-making industry of the time. She named the cheese after her farm in Denmark where she developed it. Havarti is a tangy, light-yellow, almost rindless cow's milk cheese with small irregular holes, and is typically produced in 4kg loaves which are matured for about three months. As the cheese ages, its flavour intensifies and sharpens. It is not dissimilar to the German Tilsit (page 129), itself the happy outcome of a failed attempt to make Gouda. Serve it with Sauvignon Blanc, a lightly-oaked Chardonnay or light-bodied red wine and figs, raisins or walnuts.

MYCELLA

Mycella takes its name, unromantically, from the strain of penicillin with which it is inoculated to produce the prized blue veins that contribute to its flavour. Made in deep wheels, with a browny-orange crust, Mycella is Denmark's answer to Gorgonzola (see page 94). Made from cow's milk, it is a soft full-fat cheese like Danish Blue (see opposite) but has a gentler flavour that doesn't overpower the creamy interior. Traditionally - made blue cheeses are only lightly pressed so the mould spores can work their way naturally into the cheese, but these days the spores are added during production and then the cheeses are stabbed with long stainless-steel needles to let in air in order to promote the growth of the penicillin. It tastes delicious in salads.

FACTS

Size
**20cm diameter,
10cm high**
Weight
5kg
Fat in dry matter
50-60 per cent
When eaten
all year
In the shops
all year
Uses
**cheeseboard; in
sandwiches; in salads**
Region
various

SAMSØ

In an early 19th Century bid to broaden the range of his country's native cheeses, the King of Denmark invited master cheese makers from Switzerland to come and teach Danish farmers their craft. The result was this pale yellow, pliable cheese, not dissimilar to Emmental (page 141). Named after the island of Samsø, it is a classic cheese that spawned a new generation of Danish cheeses. Made with whole pasteurized cow's milk in wheels or heavy blocks, it has a super-thin yellow rind and a pâte scattered with eyes of varying sizes. It is aged for two to six months, although the Danes seem to prefer it when it develops the delicate sweet-acid flavour of maturity. With Havarti (opposite), it is an essential ingredient of a Danish fondue.

FACTS

Size
various
Weight
14kg
Fat in dry matter
30 to 45 per cent
When eaten
all year
In the shops
all year
Uses
**cheeseboard; in sand-
wiches; for grating,
grilling and melting;
Danish fondue**
Region
various

NORWAY

Craggy mountains and dense forests almost rule out grazing in Norway. Only one per cent of Norway's skinny coastal strip is given over to cows and goats, so the odds against Norway as a cheese-producing nation are firmly stacked.

Yet Norway's cheese industry is surprisingly successful. Cheese making was brought to Norway by Benedictine monks in the 9th Century, who hoped that it might help transform the war-hungry Vikings into peaceful farmers. Almost two thousand years later, the industry is thriving.

The foreigner's favourite is Jarlsberg, with the majority being exported to the USA, but the Norwegians prefer something more eccentric. Their choice is Gjetost, an unusually sweet aromatic cheese that is not to everyone's taste.

NORWAY

GAMMELOST

The most distinctive feature of this goat's milk cheese is the greenish, brown mould that forms on its rind, which starts as a soft brownish-yellow paste with veins of blue mould running through it, but becomes extremely hard and brittle with age. Traditionally, to encourage the hardening of the rind and add to the flavour, the young cheese was wrapped in straw soaked with juniper berries. It appeared to age before its time, which led to its name, Gammelost, meaning 'old cheese'. Once inside its bitter skin, the creamy, blue cheese has a full aroma and a flavour with a sharp twist that sets the tastebuds zinging. It has an exceptionally low fat content, and is usually served after dinner with gin or aquavit.

GJETOST

Eaten with fruitcake as a Christmas treat, this honey-brown cheese - one of Norway's most popular - is sweet, with a fudge-like texture. The name derives from *gjet*, Norwegian for goat, and as it originates from the Gudbrand valley, it is also called Gudbrandsdalsost. The traditional cheese, made from pure goat's milk, is known as Ekte Gjetost, but it can also be produced using pure cow's milk, when it is called Mysost. Gjetost is made by boiling milk whey until the lactose caramelizes and browns, then pouring it into rectangular moulds before cooking. The taste is unusual: sweet, creamy and slightly sour, and not for everybody's palate. It is eaten with coffee, thinly sliced, or used in a fondue. Historically, mariners took Gjetost with them on long voyages.

JARLSBERG

Hard and creamy with holes of various sizes and a pleasant flavour, this highly popular cheese was first produced in 1815 in Oslofjord, southern Norway. Thirty years later, a professor from the University of Norway researched and revived it, combining traditional production methods with modern technology. The result was named Jarlsberg, after Count Wedel Jarlsberg, owner of the estate where the cheese was first produced. Today, Norway exports it to Canada, Australia, the EU and U.S.A., where it is one of the top-selling cheeses. Jarlsberg is based on Swiss Emmental (page 141), although it lacks the same depth, and is sweeter and less nutty. It is made from the milk of cows grazing on the high summer pastures, giving it a golden yellow colour.

RIDDER

An aromatic, full-bodied cow's milk cheese with a sweet-savoury taste, Ridder was developed in the late 1960s and is produced in a small dairy beside a picturesque fjord. Ridder translates as 'knight', which is meant to suggest the characteristically strong flavour. A solid, semi-hard cheese, it is aged for about three months in a putty rind. The result is open textured and elastic, with the buttery feel of French Saint-Paulin. The taste is slightly piquant and can turn quite sharp. It is available with a sticky, orange, washed rind, or vacuum packed. The unwashed, rinded Ridder has the sharpest taste. Ridder is excellent as a sandwich filling, snack or table cheese, and can be melted or grilled. It is popular in Japan.

SWEDEN

In the glacial Swedish winters, when isolated towns could be cut off from fresh meat, keeping cows and goats for dairy products was more than usually essential.

Once, cheese making in Sweden's small farms and dairies meant regional individuality flavoured each cheese.

Now, in common with other Scandinavian countries, Sweden is a considerable mass producer of cheese, which means less and less artisan cheese.

Although Västerbottensost is still exclusive to West Bothnia where it was invented in the mid 19th Century, older cheeses such as Hushållsost (with a 700 year old history) have been made and marketed too successfully by mass producers for traditional methods of manufacture to stay alive.

SWEDEN

Size
varies
Weight
12-18kg
Fat in dry matter
30-45 per cent
When eaten
all year
In the shops
all year
Use
cheeseboard
Region
various

HERRGÅRD

This speciality cow's milk cheese is round, with a smooth, natural rind, usually encased in yellow wax. Its name, Herrgård, translates as 'manor house', and it has a long, intense production process, which gives it an unusual mild, nutty flavour overlaid with a slight tang. It is similar to Gruyère (page 142), but is softer, more supple and has smaller, rounder holes. It melts easily and keeps well. The cheese is made with pasteurized milk, acid-producing bacteria and lactic bacteria as a starter culture. After the curd is cooked, moulded, pressed and salted, it is coated in wax and cured for seven months at 16°C. In addition to the regular cheese, there is a low-fat version, made with skimmed milk.

FACTS

Size
**20-25cm diameter,
5-8cm high**
Weight
3kg
Fat in dry matter
45 per cent
When eaten
all year
In the shops
all year
Uses
cheeseboard; in sandwiches; for grilling
Region
various

HUSHÅLLSOST

Made in Sweden for 400 years, Hushållsost translates as 'household cheese', a label that reflects its popularity with families and children. Its unassuming, mild flavour and open texture make it perfect for a breakfast cheese, sandwiches or grilling. Unlike most Swedish cheeses, which are made with skimmed milk, Hushållsost is produced with full-fat pasteurized milk. The production process is similar to that used for Serra de Estrela (page 119), and includes acid-producing bacteria and lactic bacteria as a starter culture. The cheese is cooked, moulded, pressed and salted, and takes around four months to ripen at a temperature of around 16°C. Semi-soft, mild and creamy, it has a fresh pale yellow colour, small, irregular holes and a slight, but surprising citrus flavour.

PRÄST

Since the 16th Century Präst has been nicknamed 'priest's cheese', as it was customary for Swedish farmers to donate a tenth of everything they owned to the church. This would include their finest cow's milk, and it was the priest's wife's duty to convert this milk to cheese for sale at the local market. The success of the cheese reflected not only the wife's cheese-making skill, but also the priest's popularity. Today, it is solely factory made, and is matured for two months. Both semi-hard and creamy with irregular holes, it has a strong, rich, distinctive flavour, ranging from languid and mellow to robust, sweet-sour and lactic. The rind is pale yellow covered in fine cloth and coated with yellow wax.

FACTS
Size
10cm diameter, 5-7cm high
Weight
12-15kg
Fat in dry matter
45 per cent
When eaten
all year
In the shops
all year
Use
cheeseboard
Region
various

VÄSTERBOTTENSOST

This semi-hard cow's milk cheese has been described as the pride of Sweden. Records suggest that it was first made in West Bothnia, in northern Sweden, in the second half of the 19th Century. It is usually produced in wheels, with a smooth hard, orange, waxed rind and a grainy texture. The maturing process for Västerbottensost is slower than for most cheeses: an average of 11 months is needed to ripen it and to develop its full, pungent flavour. It has been compared to Parmigiano-Reggiano (page 98) and they do both share a rich taste and have a subtle, bittersweet tang.

FACTS
Size
50cm diameter, 20cm high
Weight
17.5kg
Fat in dry matter
45 per cent
When eaten
all year
In the shops
all year
Uses
cheeseboard; for grilling and grating
Region
various

FINLAND

One third of Finland lies within the Arctic Circle, where the reindeer is superbly adapted for survival, and obligingly provides humans with food, including milk that has four times as much fat as cow's milk and a distinctly gamey flavour. This can be used in two of the three cheeses featured in the following pages.

The market is largely dominated by factory-produced cheese, but the cheeses featured here are sometimes available in 'farmhouse' versions. Perhaps the most distinctive Finnish cheese – an oddity if nothing else – is Munajuusto, made with eggs. (Ilves, another egg cheese, is no longer generally available.)

FINLAND

FACTS

Size
**10-15cm diameter,
5-7cm high**
Weight
6-10kg
Fat in dry matter
50 per cent
When eaten
all year
In the shops
all year
Use
cheeseboard
Region
various

TURUNMAA

Turunmaa derives its name from Turku, Finland's ancient capital on the south coast. It was probably introduced in the 16th Century in one of the great manor houses of the time. Made from partially skimmed cow's milk and produced as a rindless drum, it is pale yellow in colour and takes around two months to mature. The result combines many textures and flavours: although semi-hard, open and firm, it still retains a smooth and creamy taste; and despite being mild and aromatic, it has a sharp tang on the fin-ish. Turunmaa is often eaten in Finland for breakfast with fruit and bread. It has been likened to both Chisholm and the Danish Havarti (page 198), in fact it is nicknamed 'Finnish Havarti'.

FACTS

Size
10cm wide, 1-2cm high
Weight
250-500g
Fat in dry matter
31-45 per cent
When eaten
mid-summer and winter
In the shops
all year
Uses
**breakfast or dessert
with jam**
Region
various

JUUSTOLEIPÄ

The name is a compound of two Finnish words, *juusto* for cheese and *leipä* meaning bread, and gives a clue to the unique character of this cheese, which is coated in a caramel crust. After draining, the curds are pressed into a flat, wooden platter with a rim, and then grilled in front of the fire until the outer layer is crusty and toasted. The cheese is made with cows' or reindeer's milk (the latter has a richer flavour and creates cheese with a solid, earthy taste). Mostly factory made now, and ready to eat after only a few days of ripening, the cheese, beneath its crust, is light and creamy with a delicate flavour: an irresistible combination. It's popular for breakfast in Finland with fresh berries or jam.

MUNAJUUSTO

Finland, with its vast pine forests and innumerable lakes, is the origin of some remarkably fine cheese. Despite its harsh terrain and inhospitable weather (cows winter in barns), dairy farming is one of the country's most important forms of agriculture, and has been since the Middle Ages. It is in this varied landscape that the traditional creamy farmhouse cheese Munajuusto is produced.

How it's made
Muunajusto is created using a tried and tested recipe of eggs combined either with cow's or reindeer milk, which is richer. The mixture is heated until it curdles, the whey drained off, and the remaining curd pressed into hand-woven baskets. The cheese is moulded into variously sized flattened balls, after which the surface becomes speckled with brown pigments. Like Juustoleipa (opposite), it can be grilled in front of a fire before ageing.

Enjoying the cheese
The finished cheese has a fresh, sunshine-yellow colour and is firm and moist, sometimes with brown marks from the toasting. It has a taste reminiscent of custard, overlaid with a slightly charred flavour. If made with reindeer milk, it has a more gamey, earthy taste. It is often eaten as a snack.

FACTS	
Size	Region
25cm diameter, 10-12cm high	**various**
Weight	
5kg	
Fat in dry matter	
40 per cent	
When eaten	
mid summer, winter	
In the shops	
all year	
Uses	
cheeseboard; for grilling	

SPECIALIST CHEESE RETAILERS

France, above all, spoils the shopper for choice when it comes to cheese, because local markets have a tradition of superb cheese stalls; the big cities have some wonderful specialist cheese retailers and most ordinary food shops have a properly stocked cheese counter. Much the same can be said for Italy and Spain. Other countries are not always so lucky: specialist cheese retailers can be scarce because of competition from the supermarkets, so the shopper has to be content with a limited range on supermarket counters.

This list is intended simply as a starting point for specialist cheese retailers in the countries featured with larger sections in this book. It is not exhaustive, but the names here can claim to be amongst the best.

FRANCE
Roland Barthélemy in Paris can claim to be the best cheesemonger in Europe; also in Paris are **Marie-Anne Cantin** and **Androuet**. **Philippe Olivier** in Boulogne-sur-Mer, **Xavier Bourgon** in Toulouse, **Cenari** in Cannes, **Cortes** in Carpentras and **Fromagerie Maréchal** in Lyon are also among the French heavy hitters.

BRITAIN, IRELAND
Two of the best in London are **Paxton and Whitfield** and **Jeroboams**, gourmet cheesemongers that employ knowledgeable staff and stock exceptional cheeses from Britain and Europe. **Neal's Yard** (two branches) and **La Fromagerie** (two branches) are also outstanding London cheese shops. This coterie is joined in Scotland by **Iain**

Mellis (four branches). For traditionally made Irish cheese, **Sheridan's** in Dublin will not disappoint, nor will their selection of European cheeses.

ITALY

Rome's most famous cheese specialist is **Bucci Alimentari**; in Milan visit **Casa del Formaggio**, **Cucina del Cornale** or **Peck**; in Bologna, **Salsamentaria Taburini**; and in Lugano, **Bottega del Formaggio**.

SPAIN

La Paz market in Madrid is particularly well known, and Madrid cheese shop **La Boulette** is famed for its wide selection. In Barcelona, **Tutusaus** is a small but excellent artisan cheese shop.

GERMANY, AUSTRIA, SWITZERLAND

Käsespezialitäten in Freiburg, Germany, stocks cheeses from Germany and elsewhere in Europe, many of them exclusive to the shop. In Vienna, visit the **Naschmarkt**. It is a wonderful outdoor food market that sells anything and everything, including many different types of cheese. In Switzerland, **J.P. and J.A. Dufaux**, in Morges, Canton de Vaud-Suisse, is excellent.

BELGIUM

La Baratte, Brussels, stands out from the competition.

THE NETHERLANDS

Head for **De Kaasspecialist** in The Hague, a small but popular cheese shop with a wide selection and friendly staff. For something more rustic, **t Kaaswinkeltje** in Old Gouda claims to be the only store in Holland to sell exclusively farmers' cheese. **Alkmaar cheese market**, Alkmaar, is also worth seeking out.

NEW WORLD CHEESES

AUSTRALIA

Cheese	Region	Description
Grabetto	Victoria	Hard, flaky, goat's milk cheese (cheeseboard)
Heidi Gruyère (v)	Tasmania	Firm, supple, cow's milk cheese (cheeseboard/fondue/grilling)
Kangaroo Island Brie	Adelaide	Smooth, voluptuous, cow's milk cheese (cheeseboard)
King River Gold	Victoria	Smooth, washed-rind, cow's milk cheese (cheeseboard)
Meredith Blue	Victoria	Mild, creamy, cow's milk, blue cheese (cheeseboard)
Tasmania Highland Chevre Log	Tasmania	Lemony, moist, goat's milk cheese (cheeseboard/grilling)
Timboon Brie	Victoria	Intensely-flavoured, cow's milk cheese (cheeseboard)
Washed Rind	Victoria	Semi-soft, pungent, cow's milk cheese (cheeseboard)
Woodside Cabecou	Adelaide	Soft, mousse-like, goat's milk cheese (cheeseboard)
Yarra Valley Pyramid	Victoria	Firm, slightly salty, goat's milk cheese (cheeseboard)

New Zealand

Cheese	Region	Description
Bleu de Montange	Various	Smooth, tangy, cow's milk, blue cheese (cheeseboard)
Brick (v)	Wellington	Semi-soft, pungent, cow's milk cheese (cheeseboard)
Evansdale Farmhouse Brie (v)	South Island	Smooth, creamy, cow's milk cheese (cheeseboard)
Four Herb Gouda Hipi Iti (v)	Christ Church	Rich, nutty, hard, cow's milk cheese (cheeseboard)
Kikorangi (v)	Wellington	Creamy, piquant, cow's milk, blue cheese (cheeseboard)
Mahoe Aged Gouda (v)	Kerikeri	Firm, slightly fruity, cow's milk cheese (cheeseboard)
Mercer Gouda	Hamilton	Unpasteurised, pungent, cow's-milk cheese (cheeseboard)
Meyer Vintage Gouda	Hamilton	Smooth, slightly fruity, cow's-milk cheese (cheeseboard)
Saratoga (v)	Masterton	Moist, mousse-like, goat's milk cheese (cheeseboard/grilling/salads/pastries)
Waimata Farmhouse Blue	Gisbourne	Creamy, tangy, cow's milk, blue cheese (cheeseboard/salads/sauces)
Whitestone Farmhouse (v)	Oamaru	Moist, crumbly, cow's milk cheese (cheeseboard)

USA

Cheese	Region	Description
Bergere Blue	New York	Roquefort-style, sheep's milk, blue cheese (cheeseboard/salads)
Brier Run	West Virginia	Creamy, semi-soft, goat's milk cheese (cheeseboard/grilling)
Bulk Farm	California	Various cow's milk, European-style cheeses (cheeseboard/grating/grilling)
Capriole Banon	Indiana	Aromatic, goat's milk cheese (cheeseboard)
Crowley	Vermont	Semi-hard, Cheddar-style, cow's milk cheese (cheeseboard/grating/grilling)
Dry Jack (v)	California	Full-bodied, hard, cow's milk cheese (cheeseboard/grating/salads)
Grafton Village Cheddar	Vermont	Unpasteurised, hard, cow's milk cheese (cheeseboard/grilling/grating/sauces)
Hubbardston Blue Cow	Massachusetts	Gently-flavoured, cow's milk, blue cheese (cheeseboard)
Idaho Goatster	Idaho	Hard, Pecorino-style, goat's milk cheese (cheeseboard/grating)
Laura Chenel's Chevre	California	Subtle-flavoured, goat's milk cheese (cheeseboard)
Maytag Blue	Iowa	Piquant, crumbly, cow's milk, blue cheese (cheeseboard)
Mossholder Cheese	Wisconsin	Semi-soft, pungent, cow's milk cheese (cheeseboard/grilling)

Peekskill Pyramid	New York	Creamy, buttery, cow's milk cheese (cheeseboard/snacks)
Plymouth Cheese	Vermont	Unpasteurised, fruity, hard, cow's milk cheese (cheeseboard/melting/baking)
Sally Jackson Cheeses	Washington	Mild, nutty, sheep and goat's-milk cheeses (cheeseboard/cooking)
Sea Stars Goat Cheeses	California	Mild, creamy, goat's milk cheese, garnished with edible flowers (cheeseboard)
Teleme (v)	California	Aromatic, semi-soft, goat's milk cheeses (cheeseboard/salads/baking)
Toscana (v)	California	Earthy, Pecorino-style, sheep's-milk cheese (cheeseboard/grating)
Vermont Shepherd	Vermont	Smooth, nutty, hard, sheep's-milk cheese (cheeseboard/grating)
Yerba Santa Shepherd	California	Dry. flaky, hard, goat's milk cheese (cheeseboard/cooking)

INDEX